The Amazing Fact
of Quaker Worship

The Amazing Fact
of Quaker Worship

George H Gorman

QUAKERbooks

First published May 1973
Reprinted January 1975
Reprinted September 1979
Reprinted May 1988
Rprinted December 1993
Reprinted January 2008 by Quaker Books

ISBN 978 0 901689 84 9

Cover photograph: Mike Hoyle
Cover design: Hoop Associates
Additional typesetting: Compositions by Carn

George H. Gorman 9.12.16 – 20.2.82

George Gorman was one of the few Quakers known throughout the Religious Society of Friends in this country, and he was also known to many in Europe and North America. In any public gathering of Quakers he was sure to know a large number by name and not a few as personal friends.

George was born in London in 1916, but his more formative years were spent in Evenlode, Gloucestershire where he moved at the age of 9, when his father was appointed rector there. His secondary education was at Chipping Campden Grammar School. These early influences ensured an abiding affection for the Cotswolds. It was hoped that he would follow his father into the priesthood but George had hesitations and the idea was abandoned when his father died suddenly when George was 17. As the only bread-winner in the family he went instead to work in an insurance company in London, but later moved to the company's office in Cheltenham.

It was here that he first met Friends. His early meetings for worship are movingly described in the final chapter of this book. He quickly became involved in Young Friends both locally and nationally. With his clear knowledge of Christian insights and values, which he found excitingly re-interpreted in the Society, and his ability to speak in public and think on his feet, it seemed natural that he should become the travelling Secretary for Young Friends. He moved to Woodbrooke, a Quaker study centre in Birmingham, to widen his knowledge of Quakerism. Here he also met his future wife, Lucy, and they were married in 1945. In 1948 they moved to London where George took up the position of Assistant Secretary of the Friends Home Service Committee at Friends House, becoming the General Secretary four years later.

It is not possible to evaluate fully his 38 years of service for Friends, but it has been said that without him the Society today would be a different Society and probably a smaller one. He had a gift for personal relationships and he often told Friends 'If you wish to make a Friend first make a friend'. This capacity for friendship with a warm smiling welcome, and his skill in drafting minutes, steering the business along with a light touch, his spontaneous humour and inspiring addresses were the qualities of a well rounded, capable and infinitely caring and loving person.

He developed an understanding of the current mood in religious thinking. In his speaking he never used religious cliches, 'God talk' or sentiment. He lived at a turning point in Quaker history which he understood, and it could be said that he anticipated the 'Honest to God' debate of the 'sixties. Certainly he was able to interpret it for Friends and others.

He was a successful broadcaster, appeared on television and served on the Central Religious Advisory Committee of the BBC and IBA. He was also for a time on the Committee of his local Marriage Guidance Council and a magistrate; Vice-Chairman of his bench and Chairman of the Juvenile Panel. He looked upon these activities as helping him to be in the world and prevented him from becoming a too inward looking Quaker.

His first book, *Introducing Quakers*, published in 1969, was a brief, but very clear presentation of modern Quakerism. It has been of immense value over the years and is still a best seller, over 130,000 copies having been printed. He also wrote innumerable articles, reports, and reviews of books, films and plays for Quaker press. He was a fluent and gifted speaker blending humour and seriousness, always holding the attention of his listeners.

Having himself been drawn to the Society of Friends through a Quaker advertisement he had a particular concern for those who were discovering the Society. He developed the use of Quaker advertising and initiated weekends for enquirers at Charney Manor, a beautiful old house in Oxfordshire. These weekends are still proving to be one of the most successful ways of providing information about Quaker beliefs and practices in an informal and relaxed manner.

In some ways *The Amazing Fact of Quaker Worship* could be seen as a sequel to his earlier work, developing the theme of Quaker worship. Certainly George himself considered this book to be the culmination of his experience with Friends and with those finding the Society for the first time.

George Gorman died in 1982 while on holiday in Sicily seven weeks after retiring from his Quaker service. He left a wife and three grown up children.

CLIFFORD E. BARNARD

The above was written seven years after George's death for the 1988 reprint of this Quaker classic. It gives me great pleasure to know that the book is still in considerable demand and that a further reprint is to be made available for another generation of those discovering the Religious Society of Friends. To me it reads as freshly and is as relevant as it was when it was first published twenty years ago.

C.E.B.

January 1993

FOREWORD

The Swarthmore Lecture involves two quite distinct, although related, activities. The first is to write a short book on a chosen theme: the second is to give a fifty minute talk on this to an audience at the time of London Yearly Meeting. The lecturer is asked to interpret to Friends some aspect of their faith and work and to present to the public something of the fundamental principles of the Religious Society of Friends.

The subject I have chosen is Quaker Worship because I am convinced that this is the most precious gift Friends have to share with others. It is also something on which Quakers themselves cannot too often reflect. As soon as I started work I recognised that this theme is the easiest and the most difficult subject on which to write. The ease lies in the fact that every Quaker has first-hand experience of this subject: it is part of his life. The difficulty is that worship touches at depth the most profound experience of people.

To find the time to write I realised that I must be out of reach of my ordinary activities. I chose to go to Pendle Hill—the Quaker Center for study and worship near Philadelphia. My expectations were completely fulfilled. The supportive warmth of love extended to me by the Pendle Hill community, and the stimulus of their continued encouragement provided exactly the right atmosphere for the work I had in mind. Added to this was the daily opportunity for participation in Quaker worship at its best. It was during those meetings that I became freshly aware of the amazing nature of Quaker worship as a fundamental fact of life.

My indebtedness to my friends at Pendle Hill is part of a larger debt to countless numbers of people on whose experience I have drawn through conversations and correspondence. For Quaker worship is essentially a corporate activity, although the way in which I have written about it is my personal interpretation.

While it would be impossible to name all who have assisted me, there are some to whom I must express my thanks for their special help. The first draft of this book was read by a number of Friends including Kenneth Barnes, Alice Mary Hadfield, Harold Loukes, Edward H. Milligan, Ben Vincent and Carol Weeds. Their constructive comments and criticisms were invaluable.

My absence from my office placed an added burden on all my colleagues and I gladly acknowledge the cheerful manner in which they carried it. In particular I express my gratitude to Clifford Barnard, not only for enabling me to be away, but also for his helpful ideas for improvements in my writing, as well as the meticulous skill and care with which he has seen the book through the press. To my Secretary, Ruby Momber, I add my thanks for her patience in deciphering my MS. and typing and re-typing it.

Finally I acknowledge the continued interest and support of my wife, who not only made it easy for me to be away for three months, but, who on my return read and considered every word and trial draft of the book. It is from her more than from anyone else that I have learnt the real nature of love, and so have come to understand something of the nature of worship.

George H. Gorman

*   *   *

*To the Pendle Hill community
with affectionate gratitude.*

CONTENTS

ACKNOWLEDGEMENTS

The author and the Friends Home Service Committee gladly make acknowledgment to the following writers and publishers for their permission to quote from copyright sources: Associated Book Publishers Ltd. for the extract from *Psychology and Religion* by Stephen Spinks; The Bodley Head for the extract from *August 1914* by Alexander Solzhenitsyn; The Bannisdale Press for the extracts from *Quaker Worship* by Gladys Wilson; Constable & Co. Ltd. for the extract from *The True Wilderness* by Harry A. Williams; Mitchell Beazley Ltd. for the extract from *True Resurrection* by Harry A. Williams; James Nisbet & Co. Ltd. for the extract from *Worship* by Evelyn Underhill; Pendle Hill for the extracts from *Creative Worship and other essays* by Howard Brinton, and *The Quaker Message: a personal affirmation* by L. Hugh Doncaster; Penguin Books Ltd. for the extracts from *A Rumour of Angels* by Peter L. Berger, and *The Way of Transcendence* by Alistair Kee; A. D. Peters & Co., writers' agents, for the extract from *Essays of a Humanist* by Sir Julian Huxley; Routledge & Kegan Paul Ltd. for the extract from *The Sovereignty of Good* by Iris Murdoch; C. A. Watts & Co. Ltd. for the extracts from *The Future of Religion* by Kathleen Bliss; the SCM Press Ltd. for the extracts from *Psychology and Worship* by R. S. Lee, and *Paths in Spirituality* by John Macquarrie; James MacGibbon, literary executor, for the poem 'Not waving but drowning' by Stevie Smith; the Editor and Ann Wilson for permission to reproduce her letter to *The Friend*.

Love is the hardest Lesson in Christianity; but, for that reason, it should be most our care to learn it. *Difficilia quae Pulchra.*

Some Fruits of Solitude (c. 1690)
by William Penn

1

APPROACHING QUAKER WORSHIP

Look closely at the Quakers in any part of the world, at any point in their history from the mid-seventeenth century to the present time, and you cannot fail to notice one outstanding fact about them: their lives, both as individuals and as a group, are grounded in the activity of worship. Pause to reflect upon this, and you will probably conclude that this is not so surprising when you recall that the name Quakers adopted for themselves from the late eighteenth century is 'The Religious Society of Friends'. The word 'religious' inevitably suggests the kind of experience that would include some sort of activity that could be described as worship. But this is not always immediately apparent to everyone. Some years ago I heard a lecture on the Quakers by a Jesuit Father, who had obviously made a great effort to master his subject. Despite this he reached the astounding conclusion that he could find nothing in Quakerism that even approximated to worship! In talking to him afterwards I described a Quaker meeting for worship and his eyes lit up with astonishment. At the close of the conversation he made the cryptic comment 'what an amazing experience'!

What's so amazing about Quaker worship? It is that for over 300 years groups of ordinary people have met together in silence, without the aids of a trained leader, or of liturgy, ritual or outward sacraments. Week by week they have shared in a corporate experiment of silent, yet open worship. In it they have felt the sense of the grandeur and tragedy of life; its defeats and triumphs. They have been aware of something overwhelming: a presence, a sense of transcendence, of truth, of the love of God. By this awareness they have been held and at the same time invigorated and re-created. So they have been drawn to make a tremendous affirmation about life's essential goodness and purpose, for they have become real people.

One main purpose in writing this book is to describe, as simply as I can, the way Quakers worship, and to explain as objectively as possible, the main reason why it is so highly valued by Friends, in the hope that some of my readers may feel that worship after the manner of Friends is something that would be of value to them.

In writing in this way I hope also to fulfil my second main purpose, which is to encourage members of the Society of Friends to take a fresh look at its worship, honestly considering its strengths and weaknesses both in principle and practice. I confess to an abiding confidence in, and a love for, Quaker worship. I long to make a better use of it myself and to see it more effectively practised throughout the Society of Friends. It meets a deep need in me, and I know this is equally true for other Friends. I believe it can also meet the needs of people beyond the Society, and this should, at least, create in Quakers the wish to share its benefits, at their best, with them.

Origins of worship

But the very sound of the words 'religious' and 'worship' is liable to put off many people today, or in some cases to provoke a violent reaction. This is because these words have become associated, in the modern mind, with an outlook on life that is thought to be no longer tenable or relevant. They carry overtones of magic and superstition—hangovers from primitive times when mankind sought to win the favour of, or stave off the anger of the gods, who they believed, arbitrarily controlled their lives. I hope that any readers of this book who are inclined to respond in this way to the very notion of worship, will be willing to judge worship after the manner of Friends as it is now, and not to prejudge it too readily from the standpoint of the primitive origin of the activity of worship. This hope applies equally to all the modern expression of worship, for Quakers have no monopoly of it.

Quakers are fully aware of the nature of the origins of religion and of its development through the long history of the human race, in which the element of worship has always been present. We would willingly, if sadly, admit that, all too frequently the variety of ways in which the religious instinct has expressed itself have been, not only disastrous, but also quite horrifying. They have included behaviour that must be unhesitatingly condemned as outrageous.

At the same time, while not in any way seeking to justify, condone or explain the evil aspects in the history and practice of religion, Quakers also recognize, thankfully, the enormous benefits for mankind that have resulted from a religious attitude to life and the practice of worship. Furthermore, we should not be true to our present experience if we did not joyfully affirm that, looking at the world from a religious standpoint together with our regular participation in worship are, for us, vital, fundamental and indispensable aspects of our lives.

I know of nothing more likely to clear one's mind and to sharpen one's practice than attempts to present an account of Quakerism to people who know little or nothing of it, and may also have only a slight acquaintance with any religious ideas or possibly a strong resistance to them. One barrier that prevents communication is the language we use. This is much loved by Friends because of the rich experience it reflects: but it cannot be emphasized too strongly that it is experience that matters.

In this opening section I shall avoid as far as possible the use of words that, because of their emotive character, are likely to cause negative reactions in the very people we wish to approach. Later, when we have had the opportunity of looking at these words more carefully, and in the perspective of Quaker experience as a whole, we will probably find that there is no other language that more adequately conveys our meaning. I have in mind such words as God, Christ, Holy Spirit, and prayer. If it were possible I should like to add the words worship and religious to the list.

In seeking to avoid their use I realize that I shall be open to criticism from readers with religious convictions because they will, justifiably, feel that I have grossly understated the powerful meaning and place of worship in their experience. On the other hand, I shall equally be open to criticism from readers with a bias towards agnosticism for appearing to 'humanize' Quaker worship by playing down its religious element.

Modern criticisms

One of the strongest and most persistent criticisms of the religious attitude at the present time comes from the sociologists. In 1967 Peter Berger, a prominent American sociologist, wrote a book to which he gave the title *The Sacred Canopy— elements of a sociological theory of religion*. This, he says, was a theoretical work which could easily be read as a counsel of despair for religion in the modern world. Both as a sociologist, and as a Christian, he became uneasy about the effects of his book, and he therefore wrote a new one 'addressed to anyone with a concern for religious questions and the willingness to think about them systematically'. He called his new book *A Rumour of Angels—modern society and the rediscovery of the supernatural*.[1] In it he pulls no punches in presenting the force of the sociological attack on religion, but he also points to a variety of factors which he describes as 'signals of transcendence within the empirically given human situation.'[2]

He invites those concerned with theological thought to seek for

4

such 'signals of transcendence' for they are 'phenomena that are to be found within the domain of our natural reality but that appear to point beyond that reality'.[3]

He adds that he is not using the word 'transcendence' in a technical philosophical sense but literally, as the transcending of the normal everyday world. We shall consider later the five signals of transcendence, selected by Peter Berger. In order to seek for such signals, which are pointers to a religious interpretation of the human situation, Peter Berger feels that emphasis should be placed on an approach to faith that he describes as induction. By induction he means 'any process of thought that begins with experience',[4] as opposed to the reverse process of 'deduction', which begins with ideas that precede experience. Peter Berger suggests that 'inductive faith' is 'a religious process of thought that begins with the facts of human experience',[5] and moves from this experience to statements about God. Whereas ' "deductive faith" begins with certain assumptions (notably assumptions about divine revelation) that cannot be tested by experience',[6] and moves from statements about God to interpretations of human experience.

In my approach to Quaker worship I am attempting to follow, as far as I can, Peter Berger's invitation, and to look at it, in the first place, as a religious activity but firmly from the standpoint of human experience. I would therefore ask all my readers, as far as they can, to suspend for the moment all their preconceived ideas about the activity which constitutes Quaker worship, and to try to concentrate upon those features most likely to be obvious to an open-minded newcomer approaching it essentially from the viewpoint of human experience.

Open to all

Unfortunately, there is a widespread idea outside the Society of Friends that participation in Quaker worship is confined to members of the Society. I cannot say too forcefully that this is an entirely erroneous view. Quaker meetings for worship are open to anyone who desires to share in them. This welcome applies equally to members of other churches or religious groups, who may, from time to time, wish to share in Quaker worship. It also applies to people who have, for one reason or another, become disenchanted with the worship they have previously experienced, yet who still feel the need for some kind of religious practice. Quakers also welcome to their meetings people who have great hesitation in saying that there is anything in their experience that could be called religious, yet are seeking for something which will bring a new dimension to their lives, that will enlarge their vision and sustain them.

The openness of Quaker worship implied in this broad welcome is the obvious outcome of an attitude of tolerance deeply embedded in Quakerism. It reflects a real sensitivity to the thought, ideas and feelings of other people. At the same time it asks them to come to a Quaker meeting with a similar openness and respect for Quaker convictions and experience. For the Society of Friends is not a vague grouping of people who, broadly, like one another and share roughly similar ideas, but who otherwise 'do their own thing' in matters of faith and action.

Interpretation of experience

Rather it is a body of people who look at their experience of the world and feel obliged to interpret it in a particular way. The act of interpretation is not static but dynamic and growing. It can be as wide as the whole gamut of life. It will take into account what has been true and real for Friends and other people of faith in previous generations, such, for example, as those of the Bible, as well as including the insights of present day Quakers into the deep meaning of life.

Having made their interpretation, Friends recognize that, in so far as the vision of life's potential and possibilities that is disclosed has about it the ring of truth, it makes demands upon them and calls for their response, both as individuals and as a corporate body. Friends therefore seek to commit themselves to it, and try to live in its light. So throughout its history the Society of Friends has enjoyed a corporate experience which, at the same time, allows a maximum freedom to its individual members.

This concept of a strong, sustaining, group experience, coupled with individual freedom, is not always an easy one to grasp, but I hope its meaning will gradually become clearer in the course of this book. It is perfectly exemplified in the Quaker way of worship and certainly to understand Quaker worship is to understand the Society of Friends. Here one comes up against the problem of attempting to put into words what is, in fact, beyond the power of words to describe. For in a real sense it is impossible to write in any adequate way about Quaker worship, just as it is impossible to describe fully the inner meaning of a loving relationship between people, or the impact of listening to great music. The only way of entering into a meaningful understanding of such deep human experiences is actually to experience them.

The difficulty of writing about Quaker worship is further heightened by the fact that it involves, as does all worship, the total response of the whole personality of those sharing in it. The attempt to analyse worship tends to cheapen the experience. Ideally, it requires one immediate expression of everything that needs to be said. But this is obviously impossible and we must look at it, piece by piece, remembering always that the whole experience of worship is always greater than the sum of its parts.

A typical meeting

The first step in this process is to sketch a picture in words of a typical Quaker meeting for worship as it is likely to appear to an

2

observer coming freshly to it. Having said this, I often wonder whether there is such a thing as a typical Quaker meeting; for meetings, like families, are composed of the people who belong to them. The word family conjures up some basic ideas of what it is, but each particular family creates its own life with its special flavour, just because it is a living organism. So no family is exactly like any other. This also tends to be true of the accommodation in which it dwells; although constructed from the same common materials, the physical fabric of any home somehow carries the characteristic stamp of those who live in it. Much the same applies to Quaker meeting houses, and to the family of Friends which uses them.

A Quaker meeting can be held anywhere for it does not require a special place consecrated for the purpose of worship. In fact, in the early days of the Quaker movement, Quaker meetings were frequently held in barns, farmhouse kitchens, or in the open air. Today most meetings take place in properties owned by the Society of Friends. Some of these are buildings erected in the seventeenth, eighteenth and early nineteenth centuries, and represent the modes of architecture typical of those periods. Consequently they have a beauty and simplicity of design that reflect the beauty and simplicity of Quaker worship. Not always so aesthetically pleasing are those meeting houses built during the later Victorian period or in the early years of this century. More recently some exciting new meeting houses are coming into existence. There is a growing practice of adapting a variety of buildings for the purposes of a Friends meeting house. Many newly established meetings have no property of their own, but rent suitable accommodation in any convenient place available. It should be noted here that Friends are acutely sensitive to the present widespread shortage of domestic housing and further reference will be made to this issue later in this book.

My main concern at this point is to establish the fact that the one basic need for every Quaker meeting is for an adequately sized room in which people can be gathered together at regular intervals.

The room itself will be simply furnished—probably with benches if the meeting house is an old building, or with chairs if it is modern. The seating is so arranged that it roughly forms a square or circle so that people can sit facing one another. There will generally be a table in the central space with perhaps flowers and a Bible upon it. The prime aim is to achieve a meeting place which allows people to sit naturally together in reasonable comfort. The first thing likely to strike the newcomer is the absence of any of the usual furnishings associated with places of worship. The meeting room has no altar, pulpit, lectern, font or organ.

Simplicity of procedure

The procedure of a Quaker meeting is as simple as the room in which it meets. As there is no liturgy or programmed order of service with hymns, set prayers and readings; so no prayer or hymn books are required. There is no priest or minister to conduct or lead the worship, for these are responsibilities shared by all who are present. No outward sign marks the beginning of the meetings: it starts when the first person arrives, enters the room and sits down in silence. Gradually other people come in, and, sitting anywhere, they too share in the stillness. Many meetings ask one, or more, of their members to act as doorkeepers, whose chief function is to give a brief welcome to people as they arrive. If a stranger feels uncertain about where to sit the doorkeeper will gladly advise him.

So meetings assemble. They can vary in size from extremely small groups comprising a very few people, to quite large ones. Most meetings are held on Sundays, and usually in the morning, this being the most convenient day and time for people to attend.

But a meeting for worship can be held on any day of the week, and at any time of the day. The most obvious aspect to impress the newcomer is the fact that they are held in silence. This is one of the unique features of Quaker worship and constitutes such a vital part of it that it must be looked at in some detail in the next section: but it is not possible to delay all reference to it now, for worshipping through waiting in the silence is the most precious heritage from our past and our most valued possession in the present.

Corporate silence

In a good meeting, and not all meetings achieve their ideal, the individuals present become growingly quietened in their bodies and minds as they sit in the stillness. People who have entered the room as individuals sooner or later become aware that they are encountering others present at a level deeper than normal conscious communication. While they remain fully themselves they also become, in a real sense, one group; a communion of people bonded together in spirit.

A pointer to this state can be seen when, for example, a small group of people drawn together by some common interest are struggling to resolve a particular problem. For some time the solution evades them: suddenly a break through is made, unity is reached, and a sense of oneness pervades the group. One of the amazing things is that, in a Quaker meeting, a far deeper awareness of unity can be reached without a word necessarily being spoken.

No one can say at what precise moment this happens, but that it can, and does happen, has been known by Quakers throughout their history. The only outward sign of it is a greater depth of silence, the intensity of which may literally be felt, for all restlessness has been stilled. When this point has been reached the group has become a 'gathered meeting', and a new dimension colours its corporate life. There is a stronger sense that the experience everyone has been sharing transcends ordinary life, while still firmly locked into it. It has about it an eternal quality that diminishes the limitations of time and space. In one way it is the creation of those present; in another it is something given to them. We shall look later at the meaning of this experience and the ways in which Quakers have tried to describe, interpret and respond to it.

For the moment we must return to our newcomer and his likely impressions of a Quaker meeting. He may feel immediately at home in the quietness and know, instinctively, that this is the natural form of worship for him. Others may feel that they are comfortable with the silence for some of the time, but have periods when they are restless and distracted. Still others, while genuinely attracted to the idea of silence as the basis for worship, yet find the practice of it extremely difficult.

Some immediate things can be said for the comfort of such people. Their difficulties may have arisen because the meeting itself did not become truly gathered, and, in such circumstances, even the most experienced Friend does, from time to time, find it difficult to be truly still throughout the whole of a meeting. Many Friends also say that it took them months to be absolutely at ease in the silence.

A difficulty common to the newcomer, as well as to Friends themselves, is that of breaking out of personal isolation into a complete sharing in the corporate life of the meeting. It is perfectly possible and valid for people to attend Quaker meetings, to be at peace in the silence, and to use them as opportunities for individual meditation. But I feel they miss the richness that comes through an identification with others in communion, which is the meeting's life. But in most people's early participation in Quaker worship they catch glimpses, however brief, of the possibilities of total involvement with others in the silence,

11

which point to something that far transcends their solitary experience, and gives hope that, with patience and persistence, they will come to expect this as a regular feature of Quaker worship.

It must also be said that for many Quakers the process I have described is reversed. They come to meeting with a vivid awareness of this sense of transcendence, or at the least with a strong expectation that it will be theirs. It will certainly be heightened during meeting. It is this that enables them to achieve a loving fellowship with the people present. Others will find a more accurate account of their experience in the recognition that it is a mixture of both these approaches, and that they vary for them from time to time.

Spoken contributions

So far I have written only of the silence that will be so obvious to the person coming for the first time to a Quaker meeting. But there is another important feature that will strike him. While on some occasions a Quaker meeting will be held entirely in silence, more often than not, there will be spoken contributions. These, ideally, should always arise out of the gathered life of the meeting, and have as their aim the deepening of that life and worship. They may take a variety of forms. The most common of these is for someone to share with the meeting an experience or thought that he has had, that has illuminated life's meaning and purpose, and that he feels will help others present to a similar awareness. Or the spoken contribution may be a reading from the Bible, or some other book. The offering of prayer is the third form in which words may be spoken in meeting, though this practice is much less frequent than in former times.

Any man or woman, boy or girl, whether a Friend or not, is free and welcome to speak in a meeting for worship, provided always that the speaking is in response to the spirit in the meeting. It is impossible to forecast how many or how few, or whether any, spoken contributions will arise, for this form of worship is extremely flexible, and spontaneity is one of its characteristics. The words spoken, if they are truly created within the life of the meeting, will sink into the pool of silence, and will help all present to plumb its depths. What is said inevitably affects the development of the meeting for good or ill. The question of when to speak or not to speak will occupy us in another section, but, as in the case of silence, something must be said now in order to fill in our picture of a Quaker meeting.

I propose, at this point, to focus attention upon the impact words said in meeting are likely to have upon a newcomer. He will notice that close attention is given to vocal contributions, and he may find that he is deeply moved and inspired by them: possibly as much by the sincerity with which they are uttered, as by the actual ideas themselves or the way they are presented. Quakers are not greatly impressed by oratory for they have not met to listen to carefully prepared and beautifully delivered sermons. Experience shows that some of the most valuable utterances are those given falteringly and without any clearly obvious sequence. Of course, some who speak have a natural facility in the use of language, and it is a delight to hear them. But of far greater importance is the experience that lies behind the words themselves. When words in meeting reflect what a person feels in the depth of his being, as well as what he knows with his intellect, then they are likely to 'speak to the condition' of those who hear them.

Sadly, this is not always the case. A spoken contribution may disrupt the silence and jar upon the ears of the listeners. One's immediate and natural reaction will be a strong sense of irritation, if not outright annoyance, that the tranquillity of the stillness has been broken. This may be a quite justified reaction, but equally it may be a misleading one. The Society of Friends has long advised those who worship after the manner of Friends to listen sympathetically to anything said in meeting, and to try to wrest from the words their inner meaning and real significance.

However, with the best will in the world, and any amount of discipline and charity, it is sometimes impossible to accept what is said, in part or in whole, as in any way useful to oneself; in that case just take from it what you can. If you are unable to find anything of value, and the speaker's unabated flow of words smothers the silence for you, then you may find it helpful to ask yourself why his message is not reaching you, or is causing such a negative reaction. Questioning yourself in this way may well spark off something that is creative in you. In fact, you will possibly come to see that the words you have been hearing with irritation do, after all, have something for you. Meetings are not always tranquil throughout. What is said may rightly challenge and disturb.

The important thing is to try to prevent a spirit of argument creeping into your mind. The most pitiable state into which a meeting for worship can degenerate is to that of a debating society. Discussion, debate and argument have their rightful place in the total life of the Society of Friends: that place is certainly not in the meeting for worship.

Having struck this rather gloomy note, which must be sounded in any honest account of Quaker worship, we can now return to Quaker worship at its best by mentioning something that is frequently true of our meetings. Words said in meeting, which may not have been helpful to one person, often turn out to be exactly what another needed to hear. It is also by no means unknown for one's mind to be groping after an idea which refuses to become clear, when someone else will express the same idea with greater clarity and fuller meaning.

The close of meeting

So the meeting continues for about an hour, although in the early days of the Society, meetings for worship often lasted much longer. The end of the meeting is formally marked by two Friends shaking hands with one another. How do these two Friends (Elders we call them, see p. 132) know that the meeting has, in fact, ended? As one would expect, there is no infallible rule that they can follow, and occasionally they misjudge the situation. Awareness that a meeting is ended is something in the nature of an intuition, although undoubtedly the clock has a hand in it. The best parallel to my mind can be drawn from the experience of an ordinary meeting between two people who are close personal friends. They delightedly encounter one another, they communicate with each other through speech, and in natural pauses of living silence. Finally, they instinctively know that the time has come to part. They may express their parting in a variety of ways, one of which could be to shake hands. They leave one another imperceptibly enriched and changed by their encounter, although this awareness may only come to them with hindsight, as they look back on the time during which they were together.

So with a Quaker meeting the group meets together, becomes gathered and achieves a corporate life and communion; so, too, the group knows almost instinctively when the time for parting has come, although there will be no strong outward sign of this apart, perhaps, from a gentle restlessness.

Before rounding off this sketch with some brief indications of the kind of impact that quiet worship has made on people experiencing their first acquaintance with it, there are a few matters to which short reference should be made, some of which must be taken up again later. One is the extremely important place children occupy in the general community of Friends. They are, of course, welcome in meeting for worship, and their

15

presence greatly enriches the total experience of the meeting. It is usual for young children to attend for ten to fifteen minutes, either at the start or towards the close of the meeting. For the remainder of the time they will be in their own groups somewhere else on the premises.

Immediately after the meeting has broken up, a Friend, who serves as its secretary (we call them Clerks), will give out any notices that will be of interest to people present, first expressing the meeting's welcome to any visitors. One or two other Friends may report on Quaker, or other activities that have taken place, or are planned for the future. It is not the practice of Quakers to take collections during or after meetings for worship. Many, however, provide the opportunity for gifts to a particular cause with which people may feel in sympathy by placing a collection box, not too obtrusively, near the door.

At the close of meeting the newcomer should do what he feels is most natural to him. He may want to slip quietly away so that he can most easily assimilate the impact that the meeting has made on him. Friends will respect his feelings and will not badger him to stay talking, although they would hope that he would be willing to accept the briefest personal welcome from one of their number. Alternatively, he may wish to meet some of the people with whom he has been worshipping. For the confident person this presents no difficulty. He will find that members of the meeting are most happy to make his acquaintance, and, I would hope, take the initiative in approaching him. For the shy person, who has difficulties in meeting people, I can readily understand that the prospect of being introduced to a number of strangers in quick succession, is quite an ordeal. But be reassured, Friends are really friendly people who will be sensitive to such feelings. The visitor should tell anyone near him that this is his first time in a Quaker meeting, and that he would like to be introduced to one or two people. If anyone wants to find out more about the meeting and its activities, again Friends will be responsive to enquiries. Elders and Overseers of the meeting (Friends appointed to care for its well-being) will be delighted to help people to find out what they want to know, and to show them books and pamphlets which may provide some of the answers to their questions. Most meetings have a visitors' book so that the people signing it can be kept informed of future activities. It hardly needs to be said that Quaker meetings are not 'dressy' occasions. People wear the clothes in which they feel most natural and comfortable.

First reactions

Many people immediately following their first Quaker meeting often say that they had anticipated that the hour would drag slowly by. Having sat through a meeting exactly the contrary has generally been their experience; they are amazed by the swift passage of time and have been largely unaware of its passing. But it is always unwise to make sweeping generalizations about people's reactions to a quiet Quaker meeting. These can vary as greatly as the people present.

For some, one meeting is enough to convince them that this way of worship is not for them. This view was succinctly expressed by a relative of mine, who declared after her first and only attendance at meeting. 'I might just as well have stayed at home and done my knitting!' In complete contrast were the words of a naval officer, who frankly admitted that he had gone to meeting convinced that it was sentimental nonsense. Leaving it, he declared, 'It kicked me in the guts!' a phrase vividly describing what had so unexpectedly happened to him.

These two comments illustrate extreme poles of feeling produced by participation, for the first time, in a Quaker meeting. A more normal reaction lies somewhere between them, as that of a young man, who, when staying with some

17

Friends was asked 'if I would like to go to meeting. No pressure was exerted and I went. I was impressed by something I know not what'. In similar vein a woman commented, 'I knew instinctively that I had come home—this was where I wanted to be'. A far stronger reaction comes from an older person who came across Quakerism at a time in his life of 'mellow atheism'. He happened to be passing a Friends meeting house one Sunday morning and went in. He was immediately struck by the silence, 'It seemed like a generated silence . . . I felt as though it began with the entire meeting, spread throughout the room, then returned to me somehow reinforced'. Writing of the total impact of the meeting he adds, 'It was like a new beginning of life. I felt unafraid and it seemed as though I had shed a fear that I was previously unaware of'.

There is probably no other element in Quaker faith and practice that commands such unanimous conviction among Friends as meeting for worship. Indeed, it commands such conviction, that they have not felt the need to defend it or explain it. But in the humanist climate of today some defence and explanation is necessary. I hope from what I have written by way of a sketch of the outline of Quaker worship that its essential simplicity is obvious. But however simple it appears, it raises penetrating and far-reaching questions regarding the nature and validity of the activity of worship and the meaning and purpose of life. It is to these questions that we must now turn our attention by a consideration of silence as the basis of worship.

II

THE ROLE OF SILENCE*

To the casual observer, looking at a Quaker meeting from the outside, it may well appear to be a strange, extraordinary and even a stupid way for people to spend their time. For here is a group of people sitting together, saying nothing and also, apparently, doing nothing. Some fisher folk of a West of England village once graphically expressed this 'common sense' point of view in their own down to earth manner: 'They Quakers just came here and sat and sat and nobody never said nothing, until at last they all died and so they gave it up.'[7]

Devoted as the first Quakers were to the value of silence, they also recognized that sitting quietly saying nothing was not exactly a normal thing for people to do. George Fox, the founder of the Society of Friends in the seventeenth century, was clear about this when he wrote, 'It is a strange Life for you to come to be Silent; you must come into a new world'.[8] This sense of strangeness was echoed by Robert Barclay, another prominent early Quaker, who stated that ' . . . there can be nothing more opposite to the natural will and wisdom of men than this silent waiting upon God'.[9]

Assault against silence

William Penn, had he lived in modern Pennsylvania, might well have felt even more strongly about opposition to silence of the 'will and wisdom' of men. For at this moment I happen to

---

* I gladly acknowledge my indebtedness to Monica Furlong's *Contemplating Now* (Hodder, 1971) which greatly influenced much of my writing of this section.

be writing in the peaceful countryside not far from the city of Philadelphia that he established 300 years ago. I am frequently aware of the shattering roar of jets flying in and out of the airport some few miles away, coupled with the rattle of trains on the nearby railway tracks: sounds sadly representative of our present propensity for creating excessive noise. A generation ago, Aldous Huxley described this unfortunate achievement of the twentieth century, and the situation has worsened since he wrote, 'Physical noise, mental noise and noise of desire—we hold history's record for all of them. And no wonder; for all the resources of our almost miraculous technology have been thrown into the current assault against silence'.[10] We may be thankful that our generation is becoming alerted to the injurious effect of excessive noise on both mental and physical health, and is slowly bringing the resources of science and technology to resolve the problem.

The healing power of silence

In a time more peaceful than ours, Charles Lamb, the eighteenth-century essayist, stumbled upon a partial antidote to his experience of the 'assault against silence'. He writes: ' . . . when the spirit is sore fretted, even tired to sickness of the janglings and nonsense-noises of the world, what a balm and a solace it is to go and seat yourself for a quiet half-hour upon some undisputed corner of a bench, among the gentle Quakers!'. This tranquil effect seemed to him to be produced by the fact that, 'although frequently the meeting is broken up without a word having been spoken . . . the mind has been fed. You go away with a sermon not made with hands . . . you have bathed in silence'.[11]

This personal discovery of the healing power of silence by Charles Lamb, who for all his admiration of Quaker worship never became a Friend, was well known to the first Friends.

Their sense that it was unnatural to people was largely coloured by the contemporary practices of church services. These were occasions for great verbalizing in lengthy sermons, prayers and singing, some of which was of a highly polemic and enthusiastic character. This is not to say that early Quakers avoided polemics and emotion themselves. There is, however, considerable evidence that, arising from their actual experience of the practice of being still and quiet they found a way to the restoration of their mental and physical resources. This they achieved in the first place at the level of ordinary life, though it must be emphasized that they were quite unable to restrict their interpretation of its meaning to this level.

My immediate aim, however, is to recognize that their starting point was rooted in everyday individual human experience and common sense. So, writing to Lady Claypole, the daughter of Oliver Cromwell, George Fox advises her to 'be still and cool in thy own mind and spirit from thy own thoughts'.[12] This idea is extended by William Penn, who, encourages people to 'love silence even in the mind' for he adds, 'true silence is the rest of the mind; and is to the spirit, what sleep is to the body, nourishment and refreshment'.[13]

This practical and naturally sensible advice can scarcely be heard by people like ourselves living in a modern industrial, and largely urban society, so it is necessary to look at the effects on us of the perpetual accompaniment of incessant noise in which we are forced to live. We are people who can hardly ever be quiet. We travel to work with the roar of traffic in our ears, we spend our days in the presence of clanging machinery, or chattering people, and our evenings in the continuous flow of sound through the facility of broadcasting. Even in the countryside we find it difficult to avoid pollution by noise. We are conditioned by our age to be noisy, so much so that we are almost afraid to be silent.

21

The false values of modern society

Western society holds before us as a supreme virtue the achievement of material success to be obtained through the activity of hard work, which is liable to become almost an end in itself. In obedience to its demands we forget to stand still for a while and ask what it is all for, and whether we should not be paying more attention to the quality of life. Instead, we drive ourselves to the limits of our physical and spiritual capacities. We become tired and bored with our occupations: but such weariness is the sign of failure, so, in efforts to conceal this from ourselves, we camouflage the dreadful fact by plunging even more ferociously into further strenuous activity.

The pressure of life upon us drives us continuously forward at its furious pace. It is not therefore surprising that our physical and mental energy is drained and we buckle under the burdens that weigh upon us from all sides. For, while human nature is extremely tough, it has its breaking point. We long to rest and to be still, yet we are fearful of what new, and possibly terrifying, sounds we may hear in the silence.

The results of the impact of life upon us are a sad reflection on the achievements of modern society, although many of them have without doubt improved the general living conditions of people. Nevertheless, the cost of these achievements has been enormous in terms of peace of mind. We should be relaxed and free, but it is quite obvious that far too high a proportion of people are tense, unhappy and unfulfilled. Despite our engagement in the strenuous and noisy activity of life, and our frequent but casual encounters with people, moving hectically from one place to another, we are basically lonely and isolated.

Western religion has largely tended to be the ally of western society in its veneration of work as an end in itself, as it has endorsed it by adding the ingredient of perfection. It is quite alarming how many people today suffer from an obsessional quest for perfection. I am not, for one moment, denying the value and usefulness of responsible work, nor the splendour of the vision of perfection. What I am saying, is that somehow we have got these excellent things out of perspective. This can only be rediscovered by our willingness to recognize that there is a natural balance between work and rest, and, that the constant striving for perfection is probably the surest way of missing the mark altogether. We have to recognize that there is an inbuilt rhythm in life to which we need to adjust so that we can respond to its ebb and flow. Such a recognition and adjustment will come about as we stop and stand still in silence.

Learning to be still

So the hint of the unnaturalness of silence and stillness given by the Quakers in the seventeenth century is even more strongly true of our age. But it is equally true for people today, that in learning to be quiet and still, modern men will find, as did the first Friends, and those in subsequent centuries, a way to rediscovery of their identity as real people, together with a sense of the essential dignity of man, through an insight into the meaning and purpose of life, by seeing it in a new perspective from the inner depths of their being. In addition, they will find a source of courage and strength which enables them to face the struggle of human existence with joy and confidence.

No Quaker would suggest that Quaker worship, in its private or public aspects is a panacea for the ills of modern life. They would, nevertheless, want to affirm most strongly that their regular participation in silent worship is, at the very least, a vital and necessary form of therapy. By and large Quakers tend to be busy people, and you rarely find them wondering how to occupy their time. They would, however, be the first to recognize how essential it is for them to have periods of disinvolvement, even from the activities which express their continuing concern to care for people. For they would fully endorse the view of that great Roman Catholic layman Baron von Hügel, 'Christianity taught us to care, caring is the greatest thing, caring matters most'. In our disinvolvement two elements will be present. First a kind of detachment that while standing back, accepts all experience in the hope of transcending it—seeing beyond it creatively. Secondly a cessation from all mental activity so that the body and mind are as still and quiet as possible.

The Society of Friends has always encouraged its members to seek a daily opportunity to withdraw from the necessary affairs of life, and, 'in inward retirement', to renew their resources, and also to ensure that they get their priorities right. There is no hard and fast rule about how this should be done, and Friends will set about it in the manner most helpful and natural to them. Whatever method they adopt they will keep in mind the testimony of Quaker experience to the desirability of achieving the practice of silence within themselves. This, for them, has been an indispensable means of exploring the riches of the interior life. It is, of course, an individual discipline, but it has a two-fold objective. The first is to enable a person to be in touch with the inner core of his being so that his whole life may be renewed. The second is to help to prepare him to enter more fully into the corporate worship which is the central activity of the Society of Friends.

Both these objectives are shared by other religious groups, but the uniqueness of the Quaker approach lies in its emphasis on the role of silence. The first is easily identifiable as having much in common with the practice of personal prayer. This, we have already noted, is a word greatly valued by religiously minded people, though many of them find it difficult, but is also one likely to present an insuperable barrier to other people, who feel they have no understanding of religious experience. I am convinced that when those of us who adopt a religious attitude to life explain as honestly as we can what we mean when we use such language, many secularly minded people will realize that their experience is not so far removed from ours as they at first thought.

Exploring the inward life

As a way into an understanding of the nature of the silence which is the basis of Quaker worship, I will try to say something of what I mean when I talk of the exploration of the riches of the interior life. Although this has a somewhat ponderous and perhaps 'cranky' sound about it, in fact, everyone has some experience of this inner journey. We live our lives on many levels, all present and operating in various degrees all the time; some of which are conscious but most of which are unconscious. Some are rightly described as peripheral but to others we attach the word deep.

This becomes obvious when we have to make a decision of any kind. A simple example makes this clear. I wish to go out for a walk and have to decide whether or not to wear a coat and take an umbrella. In view of the uncertainties of our climate I have to give a little thought to this question. For a start, I glance out of the window and examine the sky. Previous experience will give me some idea of what to expect. If anyone else is around I shall be wise to seek his view. I may be able to recall the weather forecast, and I shall certainly take into account the approximate period that I shall be out, and also where I am going. These operations of my mind take place in quick succession: in fact, I am only dimly aware of them as they have become almost automatic responses through which I reach a decision. By no stretch of the imagination could it be said that I have engaged in a process of deep thought.

Compare what happens when I am required to make a

decision on which the whole future course of my life, and that of my family, depends. For example, should I move to a new job, though it means the children changing schools? Is it right to uproot the family—or do we all need adventure? A process, similar to the simple one just described, takes place, but on this occasion every faculty I have is brought into play so that my whole personality is involved. As I wrestle with the problem I know I am doing so at all levels, and, finally at great depth; the operation has been a journey to the interior side of my life.

When I look back upon such an exercise I may well be struck by the sense that it was at what I can only describe as the depth and centre of my being that my decision was ultimately reached, and by means that in the last resort were apparently beyond my conscious control. It may have been a decision that I instinctively, as well as consciously, recognize will involve considerable risk. At the same time I am convinced that it was not only the best kind of solution that I could find at that time, but also one that it was absolutely right for me to take. Furthermore, in a strange sense, it was ultimately given to me. So the turbulence of the long hours of intellectual struggle, discussion and argument, plus the turmoil of emotional strain are replaced by a sense of inner peace. This at one and the same time seems to transcend one's ordinary experience, yet is not separated from it.

The still centre

This fact of an awareness of a deep, still place at the centre of one's being, was vividly portrayed to me by a friend of mine who described to me his experience following a family disagreement in which he had been involved. The circumstances were quite commonplace. He and his family had gone to the country for a holiday and were staying in a small cottage. As so often happens in family life, a small difference of opinion, fanned by some pent-up emotions caused by the behaviour of the children, rapidly flared up into a first-class row. In the overcharged atmosphere tempers were lost, and a noisy slanging match ensued. In all this my friend frankly admitted that he took full part; finally he could stand it no longer, so, with a last shout at everyone, he rushed from the house slamming the door behind him.

Once outside, he walked at a fast pace towards a nearby hill, fuming vigorously about the righteousness of his cause, and the crass stupidity of his family. The higher he climbed, the more the beauty of the surrounding countryside was disclosed to him. As this penetrated his consciousness, he realized that he was being calmed by it. Finally, on the top of the hill he sat down to enjoy the sheer delight of his surroundings. Gradually a deep peace grew within him as he absorbed fully the loveliness of what his eyes were seeing—how peaceful everything was. This aroused in him a strong sense of identity with the natural things around him: he felt part of the good earth.

Inevitably he compared his present state with the recent turmoil of his family life in the valley below. Now he found himself looking at that upheaval in a new light. With some effort he recalled the events that had led to the row; how trivial they now seemed. The more he reflected upon the incident, the more he recognized his own share of responsibility for it. With deeper thought things slowly came into perspective. The quarrel was, after all, but a superficial happening—the healthy release of aggressive feelings to which all human beings are prone. He knew that the deep love and affection, which was the basis of his family life, continued unharmed by the surface explosion. Finally, he knew this truth deep inside himself, where he had discovered a quiet still centre which had become available to him when he was truly silent.

In his account of this quite normal experience, my friend

gave great weight to his response to the natural beauty of his surroundings which had been for him, on this occasion, a way into the interior of his life. Similarly, for countless numbers of people the impact upon them of the wonder of nature; its creative ingenuity, and its complex but simple beauty arouses a strong sense of identity with it. As they give themselves fully to it they inevitably discover an inward stillness, so difficult to describe in words, but such a sure part of their own reality. Francis Thompson, writing of man's awareness of his harmony with natural things says, 'Their sound is but their stir—they speak by silences'.[14] This silent speech of nature calls softly to the silence in ourselves.

The role of personal relationships

For me, and I suspect for many Friends, one of the most powerful recognitions of the journey to the interior of one's being comes through the experience of relationships with other people. From time to time, during a chance encounter with another person, I am suddenly aware of the marvel of what is happening. Before me stands a unique, unrepeatable individual, the vivid focus of countless years of the evolutionary process. A sense of awe wells up from deep inside myself; at the same time I have a sharpened sense of my own real identity. The fact that we can communicate with each other increases this profound sense of wonder.

When the individual I encounter is someone with whom I share a deep, personal, loving relationship the potential depth of communication between us is enormously intensified. We do not approach our friends with a fixed agenda in our minds of items to be discussed, although we may have certain things we specially wish to share with them. It is not unusual for a conversation to start at the level of small talk. Words flow naturally, and, gradually, more important issues occupy our attention. Little by little, and imperceptibly, the exchange of ideas and experience shifts to a deeper level, until a point is reached where language is quite inadequate to convey the richness of the communication. We fall into an easy, natural silence, but there is no break in the relationship; for it is now so profound that it is beyond the power of words to express. The communication continues and deepens in the living silence that encompasses us. It may last for a few brief moments or for a longer period: the important thing is that it happens.

Afterwards, as we reflect upon the experience, we both realize that the encounter was more than a meeting of minds, an exchange of ideas, and a sharing of views, insights and feelings. We know that each has given to the other his whole personality, and likewise has been equally open to the other. Each will know that his personality has been inevitably enriched and enlarged by the encounter that has taken place at the most profound level of our being. It has been a meeting together in life, love and being itself. So this very human event takes on a transcendent quality of which each may be dimly aware at the time, but whose full impact may not be disclosed until later. When its meaning breaks upon us we cannot help but feel a sense of awe and wonder at the mystery of human love and friendship and be warmed by its power, and filled with speechless joy at its beauty.

Our decision-making, our learning to live with our aggressive selves, our enjoyment of nature, our personal relationships, and all our ordinary and extraordinary experiences of life contain within them elements of a journey to the centre of our being in which, finally, we are still and silent. The interior life is both simple and yet complicated and mysterious. One of the noblest contributions religion has made to mankind has been through its insight into this side of our nature. Yet the strange thing about our sophisticated culture is that we still know so little of the real nature of the inner life. This is true despite years of scientific work, and the more recent knowledge available to us through depth psychology. Julian Huxley sees the need for a reappraisal of man's religious experience as part of 'a thorough investigation of man's inner world, a great project of "Mind Exploration" which could and should rival and surpass Space Exploration in interest and importance'.[15]

During its 300 odd years existence the Society of Friends has, in its own way, made a small contribution to this area of exploration by its continued emphasis on the need for man to be aware of the still centre deep in human personality. This, Quakers have known primarily in actual experience rather than through a process of reasoning. For Quakers, the cultivation of the interior life through the regular practice of periods of silence, has been an essential part of living. They know it as a way into that quiet place which is the vital core of man's being: the deep focus of his self-consciousness. It is from this centre that all creative energy radiates, and to which men must constantly return for renewal in the necessary ebb and flow of life.

The meaning of worship

My aim so far in this section has been to show that, while at first glance, the deliberate practice of silence may seem unnatural, particularly in a busy noisy age, it is, on the contrary, a most natural and indeed necessary human state. Moreover, it is part of the everyday experience of everyone, although they may not always recognize it as such. We must now consider the unique use that Quakers have made of silence by adopting it as the basis for their corporate worship. At this point some attempt must be made at a partial clarification of the word worship in order to indicate how I am using it at this stage of our consideration. In so doing I must remind my readers of

30

the deliberate limitation I have set myself in describing a typical Quaker meeting, and in the discussion of the role of silence in the lives of Friends as individuals and as a corporate body. Following the line of an inductive approach to faith I have been emphasizing the human facts of Quaker experience.

With this in mind I wish to consider first worship as an individual form of human activity, when we purposively put ourselves in the position of paying particular attention to those things in life which have the greatest meaning for us. In this sense worship is a sitting down in the presence of our values. It is an act of recollection in which we become more fully aware of their real meaning for us. By concentrating attention upon them we allow them to enter our consciousness and to become part of our actual existence. We bring them to the forefront of our minds, thus allowing them to strengthen their hold upon us, and also to adjust our perspectives.

One of the most vivid experiences of such an act on my part was sitting quietly for at least an hour before a picture by the Dutch painter Vermeer, and absorbing its sheer beauty. The gallery, in Boston, had many paintings by other artists, but this was the one I wanted to see, as my time was limited and the likelihood of my being again in that American city was remote. The room was crowded with people, but I was oblivious of them, as I was equally oblivious of the passage of time. As a result of this act of concentration the vision of this particular masterpiece is indelibly stamped on my mind which has for ever been enriched by it. I know that my ordinary acts of seeing and observation have been sharpened by that experience. There was drawn from me an acknowledgement of the greatness of the artist and his painting and I caught, with awe, the light of his inspiration and creativeness. Further, something was given to me that I can only describe as, literally, a tran-

31

scending of the normal everyday world. This quite simple secular act was for me a truly worshipful experience.

There is always a danger in giving particular instances of things that one has found helpful. Partly because our view of what is useful is so subjective and personal, and writing about it so easily becomes pretentious. Partly because the variety in human taste is so great that something of deep meaning to me is liable to be anathema to others. I fully recognize that looking at pictures in general, and seventeenth-century Dutch ones in particular, is a rarefied hobby. However, the point I am making is that, at one level, the experience of worship happens in and through a great variety of seemingly 'non-religious' events, and we may rightly use the word 'worship' to describe them. In what I have written so far I have mentioned the impact that nature makes upon many people. Clearly, contemplation of its wonders can bring them to an awareness of a transcendent quality in normal human life. Although I have no feeling for mathematics I am assured by those of my friends who are mathematicians that concentration on its concepts produces, deep in them, a reverence and a sense of awe that they express in silent wonder.

In her book *The Sovereignty of Good* Iris Murdoch carries further the idea I now have in mind as I seek to set out something of the meaning of worship. She writes, 'I think there is a place both inside and outside religion for a sort of contemplation of the good, not just by dedicated experts, but by ordinary people; an attention which is not just the planning of particular good actions but an attempt to look right away from self towards a distant transcendent perfection, a source of uncontaminated energy, a source of *new* and quite undreamt-of virtue.'[16]

Worship and personality

The act of worship must be one that involves the whole personality, and should not be restricted to the perceptions gained through our senses, and thoughts based on them. This view opens such a wide perspective that it is necessary to find a point of focus. This I believe can be found in the realm of personal relationships, and it is in them that I would look for the most adequate model (see p. 64) of worship. It is here that we are most likely to be brought to the greatest sense of those things that are true, beautiful and good. All real relationships imply a natural giving and receiving: we feel able to make demands upon our friends, knowing that at other times we shall gladly respond to their demands upon us. In our periods of difficulty and stress we naturally look to our friends for support which inevitably involves an element of sacrifice. Loving and being loved is surely an essential truth about life. It is an experience, which, more than any other, gives rise to a sense of wonder, awe and reverence. While loving relationships are so much a part of life itself, they continually transcend everyday worldly events. They constitute for me one of the supreme signals of transcendence.

We cannot escape being in relationship with people for this is the inevitable consequence of our human condition. For good or ill, our personal relationships colour our lives. At best, they liberate us and release us from fear: at worst, they produce some of the most damaging effects upon human personalities. Because some people find it hard to achieve satisfactory relationships, and, for others, their experience of them has either been severely restricted, or downright bad, we must return to this subject later. For the moment I want to emphasize the way in which a good loving relationship fulfils human destiny, and is known to us most vividly and completely in moments of silence in the depth of our being.

33

What I have said about personal acts of worship applies equally to worship with others. The starting point of every Quaker meeting is the gathering together of individuals. We bring ourselves just as we are. We offer to the meeting the gifts of our experience of living, which include the fruits of our private moments of attention and resolution gained through the silent exploration of the depths of our being.

So in meeting together for worship Quakers are, at the least, consciously setting aside a time in which they may search for and concentrate upon those values that make life worth living, and are, at the same time, also silently proclaiming their worth. As I said earlier they are making a tremendous affirmation that, despite all the signs to the contrary, life is good and something that calls for reverence. Added to this is the further, but related, affirmation concerning the supreme values of love and truth. Sitting quietly together in the presence of these values, concentrating their whole attention upon them, and opening their personalities to their influence, Quakers become people whose lives are subtly changed by the experience, and in whom new energy is created. It is, therefore, to be expected that attitudes of gratitude, thankfulness and joy arise from the company of Friends, together with the unspoken understanding that they are committed to live in willing obedience to the light that has been given to them.

From a sociological point of view it could be said that Quakers meet together for worship in order to seek the sustaining power of a support group for mutual encouragement in the beliefs they hold, against the opposition of a largely hostile world. I can see nothing in the history or present practice of the Society of Friends which would deny this judgement. At the same time I am equally sure that it only partially accounts for the value that Quakers attach to their worship. Quakers gather for worship in this communal act because,

34

through it, something more is available to them, in a different and richer form, than it is possible for them to discover in solitude.

Corporate worship

Three beautiful images, which indicate some features of this extra quality released in the act of being quietly together in worship, have come down to us from the seventeenth century. The first is from Robert Barclay, who says, 'as many candles lighted and placed in one place do greatly augment the light and make it more to shine forth, so when many are gathered together in the same life there is more of the Glory of God'.[17] In this Barclay emphasizes the corporate illumination that can arise in a gathered meeting. His contemporary, Thomas Story, draws attention to the refreshment and deep joy that early Friends found together in their meetings, for ' . . . as the many small springs and streams descending into a proper place and forming a river becomes more deep and weighty; even so thus meeting with a people gathered of the living God into a sense of the enjoyment of his divine and living presence'.[18] Finally, Isaac Penington notes the impact of people upon one another in meeting, 'for, the warmth of Life in each vessel, doth not only warm the particular, but they are like an heap of fresh and living coals, warming one another'.[19]

These simple illustrations, drawn from natural things, powerfully convey a sense of a company of people who have been illuminated, deeply refreshed and warmed by their corporate act of worship. They are as true of Quaker worship today, as in the Society's early years. Implicit in them is the dimension of creative love of which we are made aware through our experience of personal relationships. This was delightfully expressed by a modern Friend when I asked her what happened in her mind when she took her place in meeting. She replied that, more often than not, she thought how wonderful it was that there were so many people in the room she loved and who loved her. In a way, so natural to her, this Friend was stating an important principle that lies behind Quaker worship, namely that its quality and vitality are inextricably intertwined with that of the loving fellowship of the local community of Friends who are meeting for worship.

Exactly how the individual participants in a Quaker meeting become caught up into a loving communion with each other remains, ultimately, a mystery. Once again we can look for help to another seventeenth-century Friend, George Keith, who suggested that, ' . . . even if but two be together . . . the measure of life in the one, doth after a secret and unspeakable manner, reach into the measure of life in the other . . . yea, and the life in the one doth so join and unite its force and strength and virtue unto the other, that every particular feels the strength and virtue of the twofold measure of life as it were doubled within themselves, and if they be three thus gathered . . . '.[20]

It would be unwise to press Keith's arithmetic too far, because this would mean that the living power of a meeting would increase proportionally to its size, and this is just not true. What is true is that in a manner that is secret, in the sense that it is not clearly obvious to our understanding, something below the level of consciousness, but still a part of normal life, does pass between people in a Quaker meeting, when they are open to it. Many attempts have been made to account for this, such as by thinking of it in terms of telepathy, extra-sensory perception, group dynamics, Jung's theory of the collective unconscious, and so on. All these ideas, and others not included in this list, are valuable in throwing some light upon the process by which individual worshippers become so melted into one another that, they are in a real sense, a united group, one body, a living, loving fellowship, a gathered meeting. As with a deep personal relationship, the meeting for worship finally eludes our efforts at complete analysis and explanation.

In writing of the Friend whose first action in meeting is consciously to recollect the wonder of the love she received from, and gave to, so many of the people in the room, I have indicated one of the numerous ways by which it is possible to enter into the atmosphere and spirit of the activity of corporate silent worship. We shall look more closely at these when we think of the Quaker attitude to prayer and meditation.

Centring down

While there is a great variety in the ways in which individual Quakers approach their meetings for worship, they are all taking part in a common activity, broadly described by the old Quaker phrase 'centring down'. It simply means the manner in which, silently, we make our interior journey to the still centre of our being. The particular starting point chosen by each Friend will be the one that comes most naturally to him. Some, for example, will seek to come to a state of concentration by fixing their attention upon an incident in the life of Jesus or on an aspect of his teaching. Others might briefly review what has happened to them during the previous week, or anticipate a future event, and ask themselves what has been, or is likely to be, the particular significance and meaning of these things. Sometimes people come to meeting fascinated by an idea, and will spend the opening period with this in their minds, trying to see how it affects their total view of life. Still others may be deeply anxious about themselves or concerned about someone they love, or filled with delight because of some joyous experience. These will be points of focus for them. Included among these approaches will be those of the Friends who simply and immediately centre their attention upon God as the ground of their being.

These and countless other ways are the starting points for the common journey inwards. For some it will be a swift, happy passage. Others will feel much sympathy with Dag Hammarskjold's comment that 'the longest journey is the journey inward'.[21] While the exercise of centring down is not mere introspection, it does mean the willingness to allow ourselves to be vulnerable and exposed to the darkness as well as to the light within. For none of us is without the shadow side to our lives, which we skilfully repress into the unconscious.

It is amazing how many of our hard, unpleasant experiences we manage to repress, which nevertheless succeed in inhibiting and damaging our conscious lives. Some physical incapacity, or a mental or emotional inadequacy in our make-up, with which we have never come to terms, is suddenly present with us in all its painful force. The recollection of a recent snub that has wounded our pride re-opens an old and deeper wound caused by a rejection we did not face, but repressed. Our sense of loneliness, insignificance, and of being unloved and unwanted; our awareness of having lost, or never found, our real identity. In the silence, these personal incapacities, all the more potent because they have been bottled up, can hurl themselves upon us with frightening violence and hideous pain. At such moments we may long for the activity and noise of normal life, which conceals these things from our inner eyes and ears. Meeting at such times seems, and is, far from gentle and quiet, but as we accept the fact that all these things are part of us and cannot ultimately harm us, the silence begins to reveal a softer, kinder face, no longer cold but warm. Memories of happier moments flood in as we recall the love that, undeserving though we were, has been given to us, and has healed us as we recognize that we were, and are, loved and accepted just as we are, 'warts and all'. Through our pain and our love we discover that life is made up of ordinary things, and that, as part of life, we are just ordinary people, not destined to be driven by our obsessional quest for perfection and freedom from pain.

If our journey is one of darkness and near despair, we should try to remember that, however dark it is, it is always a journey towards the light. This remains true even if on particular occasions we do not find it. In meeting we have a responsibility to help one another, by being open and sensitive to the conditions of those who are gathered with us. By contributing their attitude of joy and confidence, the joyful can sustain those who are burdened. The anxious can place their trouble quietly in the growing life of the meeting and know that it will be willingly accepted: for we are a society of friends and this natural sharing is part of what real friendship means.

The gathered meeting

I said earlier (p. 10) no one can detect the exact time at which a meeting actually becomes gathered: it will depend to some extent on the facility with which each individual reaches his own still centre. One of the signs by which we may recognize this state is not only a sense of outward stillness that reflects the profound inner quietness, but also by the fact that we become more intensely aware of our individuality, coupled with an equally strong awareness of our essential relatedness to others. A comment from an Anglican writer, R. S. Lee, is helpful here: 'Group worship,' he says, 'should heighten, not lower the value of the individual . . . individuality once developed cannot be ignored without peril . . . group worship, if worship is the offering of the highest, must also move on to a new level, in which individuality and community combine to enrich each other and neither contradicts the other.'[22]

4

Each individual will be acutely aware of his 'oneness' with life itself. A Friend described this state to me as 'conscious unselfconsciousness'. It is gained more readily by some present, and this undoubtedly helps others, who are finding it more difficult to achieve. There will of course be times when someone present will simply relax, letting thoughts wander at random through his mind, but gets nothing clear out of it. He finds no centre, yet is glad to have sat quietly with his friends for a while. There should be nothing in the meeting to make him feel that he is excluded.

It is necessary now to recall what was said earlier about ordinary human friendship. During our actual encounter with the person we love we may be vaguely aware of the rich meaning of the experience. But we shall probably only be able to see its full richness and meaning at a later time. This is equally true of our meeting together in Quaker worship. In writing as I have about it, I recognize that I am only able to present this interpretation of it in such sharp focus because I am looking back over years of my own, and other Friends', experience of it.

The meeting comes to be truly gathered when most, if not all, of those present have themselves been drawn in to the very depths of themselves so that even their thoughts have been stilled and their minds, while by no means empty, are in near perfect rest. Perhaps this approximates to what mystics mean when they talk of 'contemplation'. The meeting's corporate awareness of this state may only be glimpsed for brief, fleeting moments, or may last for shorter or longer periods. Because of its nature it cannot be adequately described, it can only be silently experienced, but it can be known by its fruit, and this is a deep sense of real organic unity, so vastly different from an imposed uniformity.

Because silence is the basis of Quaker worship I have used

the word and its synonyms many times. However, we must never forget that silence, like meditation, is not an end in itself, but a means to an end. The goal of the meeting, that destiny to which it is being called, is unity. 'Silence itself' says Rufus M. Jones, 'has no magic.'[23] It can, in fact, easily become the setting for a drowsy deadness in the mere absence of sound. It should at its best, be vital and invigorating, for worship is creative work, which is absorbing but never dreary or dull, although at times it calls for real effort, but of the kind that is not exhausting, because of the rich rewards it brings.

Take it gently

Consider any activity you really enjoy doing, which fully engages your interests and gives you great satisfaction. The more you devote yourself to it in a self-imposed discipline, so much the more will you receive from it. In fact, your interest may turn out to be more truly relaxing than the conscious efforts you make to relax! One obvious feature about any such activity is that you will not be able to maintain an equally high pitch of intensity all the time. There will be moments when you need to sit back from what you are doing and rest a while, only to return with renewed vigour. However absorbing your particular interest is, there will also be moments when your attention wanders and you indulge in a spot of harmless daydreaming. When you realize what is happening you gently pull yourself back, without recriminations or feelings of guilt. Similar attitudes should guide our behaviour in meeting. We have to learn to take it gently and not to panic if we find that our concentration varies and our thoughts stray. By accepting calmly that these things will happen, we find that we can re-enter the spirit of the meeting, which in any case has been holding us all the time.

I have spoken of the growing life of the meeting, using the

name meeting as a generic term to cover all the people who have met together. It is not to my mind too fanciful to suggest that, just as the psychosomatic complex of energies that constitutes a human being has, as its focus a quiet, still centre, so also is there a still, quiet centre deep in the life of the meeting. It is into this silent, spaceless, timeless dimension that everyone present is being drawn. In my description of a typical Quaker meeting I said that although such a meeting can be held in complete silence, more often than not some spoken contributions will arise. When these have been created in the deep silent life at the heart of the meeting they will have the power to assist all to an awareness of its corporate life, and, perhaps enable those who can only sense isolation, to move gently from their lonely position into the stream of the meeting's consciousness.

However, it must be pointed out that there may always be some present whose journey to the silent inner side of their lives is likely to be a solitary one, with a minimal awareness of the presence of others. When they reach the deep central place in their own personalities, their strongest sense will be of a oneness and identity with life, rather than a clear recognition of their relatedness to others. However, as they dwell at that point, they too will know that they have finally been gathered into communion with others, in the central stillness that is beyond space or time, although always existing within space and time.

Importance of intention

On the part of each one who approaches Quaker worship, if it is to achieve its fullness, there should be the intention to give all of oneself to the adventure of the exploration of the inner life. This means that we must try to be open in love, sympathy and understanding to our own needs and inner richness. In the same spirit we should be willing to receive similar gifts from others. If someone goes to a meeting in any other way than this open, expectant attitude, it is hardly likely, although not impossible, that he will experience much of the creative wonder of silent worship.

But assuming that each person attending a meeting is willing to share fully the gift of himself, with all his human joys and griefs, achievements and bitter disappointments, his hopes and his fears, and is not afraid to make, with others, the mysterious journey to the inner side of his life, what is he likely to find? He will quickly discover that he is not alone in his varied experiences, for a meeting is likely to include people whose spiritual progress is as varied as his. Some will be in advance of him in some directions, and they will give him hope of the possibility of progress in his search. Others may have different insights or hesitations; their findings or doubts will challenge him to re-examine his position—in his turn he can help them forward.

Because of his initial openness to the possibilities of the meeting, he is likely to find himself caught up and involved in its vibrant life. He will know a stillness of body and mind, and the delight of the creative work of worship with others. There will be alternate elements of passiveness (but never flabbiness) and of rich, creative tension, in which he knows a profound stillness. For some this state is finely described by what T. S. Eliot calls, 'the still point of the turning world'.[24]

If not at the time, then certainly later, he will realize that he has had a real opportunity to grow and to be—that in losing his individual self in the group consciousness, he has, in fact, discovered his true personal identity. He comes from meeting with a new outlook on life for he has experienced a mode of life that cannot be known in ordinary busy activity. His active self is now able to function with balance and perspective, and at the same time to retain below the surface activity, a sure, certain stillness.

Such then is the role of silence and our interior life in the meeting for worship. But our account of Quaker worship cannot be left there. That seventeenth-century Friend, George Keith, indicates why in his summary of a Quaker meeting, '. . . whenever Friends came together and sat down in stillness and quietness they came to find the benefit, advantage and glory thereof in a wonderful and remarkable manner, for they became all as one body . . . yea in the silence and ceasing of all words they were inwardly refreshed, comforted, quickened and strengthened through that communion and communication of spirit and life of God . . . as from one upon all, and from all upon one'. Keith reported truly for his contemporaries in this interpretation of their experience as 'communion with the spirit and life of God'.[25] We must now consider how twentieth-century Friends interpret this experience, and express their own.

III

WHO OR WHAT DO WE WORSHIP?

It is quite obvious from the writings of seventeenth-century Quakers that they clearly saw their meetings for worship as occasions when 'they were gathered of the Living God', and were in immediate communion with his spirit. It was their conviction that it was the impact of that spirit upon them that drew them into such deep unity with one another: a unity that had its source in the unifying power of God, and gave to their common activity a numinous dimension. For it was God 'in whom they lived and moved and had their being'. God for them was not far removed, not an almighty potentate before whom they grovelled in abject fear and servile humility, but rather the divine source of a life-giving energy, healing in its warmth, and disclosed to them in the innermost depths of their being, specially as they tried to answer 'that of God' in one another.

They carried their understanding further by their recognition that there was 'that of God' in every man, whether or not people recognized it. They sharpened and personalized this awareness by claiming that it was in, and through, the life of Jesus of Nazareth, and his particular disclosure of the nature and character of God, that the full richness of God's presence in the world came to them.

In the release of Jesus from the limitations of his earthly life by the almighty power of God, so that he became identified with the eternal Christ, Friends saw the possibility for the transformation of human lives by the immediate presence of a powerful source of enlightenment and loving energy. They never tired of stressing the fact that 'Christ has come to teach his people himself'. With a boldness that shocked their fellow Christians, they 'backdated' the enlarging effects of the coming of Jesus, so that, as the eternal Christ, the benefits of his life, death and resurrection, were made available to all races of mankind, of all religions and for all times. They struggled for language adequate to describe their experience and frequently used the metaphor of light, and so spoke of the Inward Light of Christ.

Despite their emphasis on the nearness of God, indwelling by his spirit the hearts of all men as a principle within them, the first Quakers never lost sight of the fact that this same principle was that which had created and continued to sustain the universe. For them, God was not only within men, but was also beyond them as the ultimate source of creative power.

Early Quaker worship

It is little wonder then that their meetings for worship were times when this creative presence of God was so immediately and livingly among them that one of their number, Francis Howgill, could write of them as occasions when 'The Lord of heaven and earth we each found to be near at hand as we waited upon him in pure silence our minds out of all things, his heavenly presence appeared, when there was no language, tongue nor speech from any creature. The Kingdom of Heaven did gather us and catch us all, as in a net, and his Heavenly power at one time drew many hundreds to land'.[26]

One could multiply, almost without number, similar extracts from early Quaker writings as evidence of their sense of the immediate power and presence of God with them. So that they were constrained, says Robert Barclay, to meet together as a people of God, 'because so long as we are clothed with this outward tabernacle there is a necessity to the entertaining of a joint and visible fellowship, and bearing of an outward testimony for God, and seeing of the faces of one another, that we concur with our persons as well as our spirits'.[27]

Not only did early Friends feel obliged to make a public witness to their new and living awareness of God's immediate presence with them, but a deeper and more private need drew them together, often at the risk of persecution and suffering. For, says Isaac Penington, 'we wait in silence of the fleshly part, to hear what God shall be pleased to speak inwardly in our own hearts, or outwardly through others with a new tongue which he unlooseth and teacheth to speak'.[28]

The power to be found in the meetings for worship of seventeenth-century Friends is vividly described by Thomas Story. He had ridden on horseback to a meeting at Broughton in Cumberland, in company with a Friend, and for some miles they had travelled together in 'profound silence'. They arrived a little late and found the meeting 'was full gathered'. Thomas Story tells us that 'I went in among the throng of people on the forms, and sat still among them in that inward condition and mental retirement'. Someone spoke but not very helpfully, and Thomas Story ' . . . took not much notice of it . . . (for) my concern was much rather to know whether they were a people gathered under a sense of the enjoyment of the presence of God in their meetings'. 'In other words,' he says, 'whether they worshipped the true and living God, in the life and nature of Christ, the Son of God, the true and only Saviour.' It was not long before he received the answer to his question for, ' . . . after I had sat down among them, that heavenly and watery cloud overshadowing my mind brake into a sweet abounding shower of celestial rain, and the greater part of the meeting was broken together, dissolved and comforted in the same divine and holy presence and influence of the true, holy and heavenly

Lord; which was divers times repeated before the meeting ended'.[29]

Seventeenth-century religion

These descriptions by early Friends of their experiences in their meetings for worship found natural and easy expression in the religious language of their period. For they were men of their age and, as such, felt no hesitation or embarrassment in talking of God or of the things of the spirit. The thrust of the Quaker protest was not against belief in God, but against organized religion that had, in the Quaker view, placed God at one remove from people. He could only be approached through the proper and widely recognized channels: the church, her ministers and the appointed sacraments and means of grace. Against this the Quakers called for, and effectively found, an immediate access to God without, they believed, any human intervention. In this way, the Quakers claimed that God had brought them out of the darkness of a second-hand religion to the glorious light and freedom of an immediate awareness of his presence.

Neither the first Quakers, nor their religious contemporaries, for one moment doubted the reality of the existence of God, and the possibility of a real personal relationship with him. The seventeenth century was a deeply religious period in which it was normal to be a believer in God. The only argument, and it was a fierce one, was about details of the nature of the belief to be entertained and the proper way of expressing it, in worship and in daily life. In one sense Friends were a minority movement, although a rapidly growing one, but in another sense they were very much a part of a popular movement, for they could identify themselves completely with the deepest religious longings and aspirations of the whole population who believed and trusted in God.

In recent years it has often been pointed out 'that religion involves a total human response, a response to the world as we experience it'. While early Quakers would not have used this kind of language to describe their experience I believe its meaning is implicit in their religious position. In looking further for a modern way in which to sum up the religious attitudes of seventeenth-century Britain I do not think it unfair to use the words of a twentieth-century theologian. In his important and stimulating *The Way of Transcendence* Alistair Kee asks, 'What makes a way of life a religious one, and what is a religious view of the world?' He suggests that the traditional Christian answer would be 'a religious experience is an experience of God'.[30]

Alistair Kee elaborates this by saying that 'In, with and under the experience of the world there is an experience of a divine, supernatural being. I do not think Christians would be content to classify the experience of a magnificent vista as religious unless the experience were somehow also reckoned an experience of the creator of the vista. Similarly no gracious action would be regarded as of religious significance unless it was reckoned also to be either enabled by God or a response to a gracious God. It must also be stressed that without the experience of God as a "personal" (in some recognizably analogous use of the word) being, worship as it has been known throughout the centuries could not be carried on.'[31]

I believe this modern summary of the requirements generally assumed necessary if an experience of the world is to be considered a religious one, can fairly be applied to the convictions of people of the seventeenth century, including Quakers. We now have to ask to what degree this is true of Quakers today. My answer is that many of them would be in sympathy with Alistair Kee's statement, and would also be able to use words similar to those in which seventeenth-century Quakers described their experience of worship.

A twentieth-century experience

A clear example of such use can be demonstrated by a quotation from the brief section on Quaker worship in the 1972 James Backhouse Lecture given by L. Hugh Doncaster. He writes: 'Our way of worship is not just a historical accident; it is a corollary from our conviction concerning the universal Light of Christ. Believing that in every worshipper, regardless of age, learning, sex or any other human label, the promptings of God's spirit are at work, Friends meet together in entirely unprogrammed silent prayer, opening themselves to him. It is our experience that in such corporate worship . . . we are led into a depth of communion with God and with one another that is deeply meaningful and spiritually refreshing. It is a fundamental part of the Quaker message that where two or three are gathered together in the name of God, there he is in the midst of them . . . At any time and in any place they may enter into the deepest communion with God and with one another . . . '.[32]

Earlier in the same lecture Hugh Doncaster, with his accustomed clarity, states what he understands by the word God. 'By "God" I mean the Ultimate Reality behind and in existence, who (or which) gives significance and purpose to life, who gives strength and inspiration, and whose nature is revealed to us most fully in the person of Jesus. It is that kind of Spirit who claims our loyalty and who gives us strength; it is a Christian discipleship to which we are committed.'[33]

Starting with human experience

Having given this clear evidence for the continued existence in twentieth-century Quakerism of an experience of worship very similar to, if not identical with, that of the seventeenth-century Friends, may I again remind my readers of the deliberate limitation and 'low key' style of my presentation adopted in the first two sections of this book. Let me recall my reasons. I wished to avoid as far as possible religious language likely to prevent many people from allowing themselves to take an objective look at Quaker worship; either on the ground that it was a superstitious irrelevance beyond their interest or experience or, more strongly, that it evoked a violent negative reaction in their minds. I gave as a further reason for my cautious mode of approach the desire to respond to Peter Berger's plea that, in any contemporary consideration of religious activities, we should start with human experience, and seek within it 'signals of transcendence', in the hope of helping people into faith.

As far as my personal experience goes, part of me warmly responds to the seventeenth-century description of Quaker worship, and therefore equally responds to Hugh Doncaster's re-statement of that experience. But it is also true that I have difficulty in using, without qualification, the religious language with which the first Friends and also Hugh Doncaster describe their awareness of communion with God. I believe I am not alone in this and that other Friends share my hesitation: but our difficulty can be overcome by approaching our experience of worship from the starting point suggested by Peter Berger.

I am deeply convinced by my long and wide experience of Quaker meetings all over Britain, and in a number of places overseas, that there are several legitimate standpoints from which Quaker worship can be observed. I am equally convinced that, in the end they are complementary to each other, and when used with a respect for the integrity and sincerity with which they are held by various Friends, they will be seen as facets of the one truth of the corporate unity and life of the

Society, which will be the richer for the variety of convictions that are embraced by it.

The problem of God-language

But why do some Friends hesitate to speak of communion with God without wanting to make some qualification? I believe our difficulty largely turns on the words we use to describe a fundamental experience shared by all Friends. We all trust in the conviction that life has meaning and purpose: the source of this trust is in the awareness of something always stirring in man towards a creative transcendence. The difficulty that many of us feel in using God-language to describe this conviction is that it tends to imply an awareness of God as so obviously present in life in a manner that is not always true of our actual experience. God often seems to be so terribly absent. I want to emphasize the words *seems to be*, because I am convinced that the depth of meaning expressed by the phrase 'communion with God' is a reality. It can also be known by many people who at first feel it cannot be theirs because the words do not convey to them anything that they are able to identify with their own experiences.

In order to help them as well as ourselves to reach this position a fresh look is required at the nature of religious faith through the insights now available to us. My approach to this will be by way of a review of some of the reasons why people in the twentieth century have a particular problem about religious faith. Then I shall seek help from Alistair Kee's consideration of the nature of religious experience which he emphasizes is always an interpretation of human experience. But to be true to the fullness of Quaker insight we shall want to go further than Alistair Kee. I find that Peter Berger's call to seek for signals of transcendence carries us forward. I then propose to apply an extension of the ideas of both these thinkers to the way in which Quakers look at the Bible and specially to its witness to the life of Jesus. Finally I shall widen the approach to cover our experience of life in general and worship in particular.

In fairness to Alistair Kee I feel I must add at this point what is the burden of his book, from which I have quoted. It is to remove the idea that having faith in Jesus, as the one who disclosed to men the way of transcendence, involves the acceptance of God as a supernatural being in whom one must believe. I recognize that the way in which I have used his excellent summary of the normal basis of a religious experience could give a false impression of the purpose of his book. While I am not convinced by Alistair Kee's general argument I do recognize its persuasive power. He is particularly convincing when he describes the difficulty and, in many cases, the impossibility of belief in a supernatural being for modern people. I feel great sympathy with what he says.

Twentieth-century Quakers are the children of their time as much as their seventeenth-century predecessors were of their age. Although we are separated from them and their fellows by a mere 300 odd years, a minute speck of time set against the long history of mankind, yet an enormous gulf divides our way of thinking from theirs. We look at our world through entirely different eyes and from a vastly different standpoint.

The impact of modern thought

'Our world view,' says Alistair Kee, 'has been shaped by the development of modern sciences.'[34] In the seventeenth century modern science was still in its infancy, although even then demonstrating that it was an extremely lively and vigorous child. Since that time the rapid expansion of human knowledge has speeded up to the staggering velocity of today. The last 30 years or so have completely revolutionized our understanding of the natural world, of the way things are in general, and in particular of the nature of man. Branches of science have become so highly specialized that it is difficult for scientists of one discipline to keep abreast of the knowledge of those in another. As for the average man, he is only dimly aware of what is afoot and is trying desperately to assimilate new knowledge that pours upon him.

The religious position itself has been under prolonged and constant attack from all sides, and the type of simple faith of seventeenth-century men in a supernatural being with whom they could enjoy a personal, trusting relationship has been shaken to its foundations. Religious people may take a little comfort from the fact that science (and for that matter religion) tends to be more humble than was once the case, but this only slightly modifies the pressure it places on religious faith. The attack on religion is not limited to that of the physical sciences. The religious position has been steadily undermined by developments in the study of history, philosophy, psychology, sociology and other disciplines. While in many useful ways light from these quarters has helped to enlarge the religious perspective, it is nevertheless true that the overall impact has been to reduce in men the inclination or apparent need for religious faith.

The result of all this is that the position and status of religious people in the national life has completely changed since Quakers first appeared on the scene. From being among the majority who shared a widely held popular faith in God as a supernatural being, with whom it was possible to be involved in a real personal relationship, Quakers, along with other religiously minded people, have been shifted to the position of minority groups considered by the majority to hold a quaint, irrelevant, superstitious and antiquated world outlook. One, moreover, that is not even effective in motivating people

54

generally to responsible moral behaviour: an effect that was once held to justify the retention of a religious way of looking at life.

Why drag God in?

So in the mid-twentieth century the majority of people in Britain are secular in their outlook, feeling no desire or need to believe in God. One could try to account in detail for this, but I fear the exercise would be tedious. I prefer to focus what I have in mind by describing two actual encounters I had with some young people, who seemed to me to represent all that is best in the younger generation. They were deeply interested in all that was going on around them, taking an intelligent interest in politics and social affairs, and were outgoing and responsible in their attitude to life. They were serious minded, without being pompous, and full of vitality and excitement at the prospect of making a useful and satisfying contribution to the future that spread before them.

To the first, a young married couple, I sent the draft of a book I had written on *Introducing Quakers* because I wanted to know their reaction to it. I did this partly because they described themselves as agnostics, but largely because I respected their thoughtful approach to life, which was one of integrity and sincerity. They were kind enough to express general appreciation of what I had written and, in the main, went along with it. Apart from some constructively critical points, their major comment was 'But why drag God in?'

The second encounter was with a girl I met quite by chance in the Amsterdam home of some Dutch Friends with whom I was staying. She was 'baby watching' for them on the evening that I arrived. In course of general conversation we discovered that we had much in common. I was the son of a Church of England Clergyman and she was the daughter of a Dutch

5

Minister, of a rather stern and narrow outlook. We swapped stories of what it was like to be brought up as the children of ministers. We had both, as the Americans would say, 'been exposed' to the lot: family prayers twice daily, with long readings from the Bible. Regular doses of church services, not only on Sundays but at odd times throughout the week. Added to this were strong commendations to personal piety, and the rigid enforcement of a narrow moral code of conduct. The subject of sex was never mentioned except in such vague terms that it was scarcely recognizable: we both gathered, however, that it was extremely sinful. The pleasures of the world were distinctly frowned upon which naturally made them seem the more delectable. She, in particular, resented this aspect of her childhood, especially as an embargo against following the mildest dictates of fashion had been rigorously applied, and severely handicapped her social life.

It was at this point in her story that I couldn't help noticing that she was wearing a miniscule mini skirt: so she immediately explained that she was no longer a believer. It happened like this. A year or so earlier she had found herself in a position of great personal distress and difficulty. In her time of crisis she recalled that a Christian could take everything to the Lord in prayer. This she immediately did. 'Do you know what I discovered?' she asked, 'there was nothing there—the whole religious business was nothing but a tremendous hoax. So I gave up believing, and, do you know, I have been so much happier since!'

The rejection of religion

The rejection of a religious attitude by these young people seemed to turn on two main points. The first that it is quite unnecessary and irrelevant to drag the concept of God in to life in order to provide it with a sense of meaning and purpose.

Such a sense, in as far as it exists, is provided by the business of living. The second, that religion not only inhibits a full life, but also fails to fulfil its promises to provide real security when it is wanted. Religious people are just as prone to fits of depression and despair as those who hold no religious faith. Mixed in with these major objections is the embarrassing feeling that haunts intelligent people reared in a scientific age, that ideas worthy of acceptance should be subject to the possibility of verification. Religious ideas and concepts are notoriously difficult to verify in any objective manner. The embarrassment of such people is heightened by the strong suspicion that religious feelings and, especially the concept of God, are but the projection of man's desires, fears, guilts and needs. However deeply Freud may have been misunderstood he had dealt a deathly blow to popular religion by his insight.

I must confess that I have felt deeply the powerful pull of these and similar arguments which inhibit many modern people from accepting a religious attitude to life. In fact, in moments of depression and doubt I have tried my hardest to clear from my outlook any religious interpretation of experience, and to reject once and for all anything that looked remotely like a concept of God. But somehow I have never quite succeeded in doing so. I am fully aware that this may be largely due to my early upbringing—I was nurtured in a loving environment where belief in God was accepted as axiomatic. Yet this has not prevented such a radical change in my views that I think my parents, if they were alive, would find it difficult to think of me as a religious person. Nor has that same environment been able to retain the active religious interests of other members of my family.

I think it is possible that I might have been more successful in ridding myself of a religious outlook on life had I not discovered the Society of Friends. From my first acquaintance with them I was immediately attracted by the fact that Quakers did not hand you a complete spiritual package of faith, creeds and dogma, which one was asked to take whole, or leave entirely alone. For them religious experience didn't look much like what I thought to be religious at all. While the Society never disguised the fact that its corporate experience pointed to lofty ideas, and to a strong sense of the reality of God, Quakers nevertheless emphasized that the starting point of religious experience is always to be found in ordinary everyday experience. This was underlined by the fact that Quakers have never tried to draw a sharp line between what is thought to be sacred and what is considered secular.

In addition to this, Quakers placed special attention upon the value and importance of the individual. As a corollary, the human qualities we speak of as personality and the possibility of enlarging this in relationships with other individual persons, has been an integral part of the Quaker religious attitude. The concept of truth was not elevated so high as almost to disappear from the vision of earthly men: rather it has been an experience to be sought in and through daily life.

Through frank and honest conversations with a great number of Quakers young and old, and through reading the extensive literature of the Society, especially its book of *Christian Faith and Practice*, I discovered experiences widely differing from mine in practice, but nevertheless containing the same basic content and ingredients. Above all there was a continuous call to search for truth, life, love, God, call it what you will, in and through the everyday experiences of life itself. This sounds strangely like Peter Berger's description of 'inductive faith' that begins with the facts of human experience and moves from them to statements about God, by a process of looking for signals of transcendence. Looking for such signals, that are pointers to a religious interpretation of the human situation

58

has a particular attraction to those of us for whom many of the great words of religion, have, for one reason or another, ceased to be useful, living metaphors which can convey meaning about the real way things are.

Interpreting human experience

Before we look through Quaker eyes at life in this way it is necessary to pause for a while, and consider a little further what in fact is involved in looking at human experience like this, and also how we interpret what we see. Here again Alistair Kee can help us because he examines the nature of religious experience in depth. I hope that in my brief references to his book I have not distorted his approach.

Alistair Kee reflects a point made by Sehleiermacher when he writes 'that religion is to be sought in the ordinary areas of life, the central essential and common areas rather than the obscure extraordinary and even bizarre'.[35] But he goes on to point out that the important thing is how we interpret them or experience them. He says 'a religious interpretation may be true or false: more often it is a question of its degree of appropriateness. Further, the interpretation which might be appropriate in one age may be deemed inappropriate in another . . . But what must be stressed, in the midst of ever changing interpretations, is the central place of experience'.[36]

Alistair Kee examines two types of religious experience which broadly cover the whole range. The first is 'the numinous experience, the encounter with the Wholly Other involves the complex elements of *mysterium tremendum et fascinans*'[37]—an interpretation of religion forcefully expressed in the views of Schleiermacher and Rudolf Otto. The second type examined by Alistair Kee is that of mysticism. Of both types of experience he makes the following important statement. 'It is always open to people to interpret experiences in a religious manner. What is at stake is the fact that it is not necessary to interpret *any* experience in a religious manner . . . There is no direct experience of God, only experiences which are interpreted in a religious manner.'[38]

Much of what Alistair Kee is saying so lucidly, is not anything very new. The view has been widely held by theologians for many years. But it has not been widely understood by ordinary people, whether or not they have a religious frame of reference. Ask the average person what he thinks is a religious experience and he will inevitably try to think of something extraordinary, outside normal experience. I am particularly drawn to Alistair Kee's statement, as to my mind it catches succinctly the essential approach made by Quakers, even though at first glance it appears to challenge them to modify their long-held claim that in their life and worship they have direct and immediate experience of God. On reflection this will be seen to be human experience which Quakers have felt obliged to interpret in a religious manner. For Quakers have, certainly in modern times, never felt that all men must believe as they do, and therefore have been able to be tolerant of differences of religious outlook because they know that it is possible for experience to be interpreted in a variety of ways: at the same time they have been clear about the way in which they corporately feel called to interpret it.

This willingness to observe with patience and humility ordinary human experience, and to interpret it and when necessary to re-interpret it, as the basis of their religious faith, means that the Society of Friends has largely escaped from the shackles that a so-called revealed and dogmatic approach to faith is liable to impose, and has enabled the Society to enjoy the richness of variety in its religious experience.

Quaker attitude to the Bible

This has been true of the Quaker attitude to the Bible. Throughout the Society's history the scriptures of both the Old and New Testaments have been highly valued. It was said of George Fox that, if they were lost, they could have been re-written from his memory. This is probably a somewhat exaggerated claim, but it remains true that both he, and all the early Friends, in common with the people of their time, had a phenomenal knowledge of the Bible. Close acquaintance with the contents of the scriptures remained a feature of the life of the Society until the early years of this century, when it gradually began to lessen. Nowadays detailed knowledge of the Bible is far from being a common accomplishment in the Society of Friends. This is not the place to discuss the reasons for this decline nor to attempt to evaluate its effects.

The point I want to make now relates to the way in which Quakers have always viewed the Bible. It has never been considered by them to be the Word of God, in which he has infallibly revealed his nature and purposes to men. Rather the scriptures have been seen as a most important body of literature drawn together over a long period of years. It consists of extremely honest accounts of human behaviour at its best and at its worst, and is therefore a unique assembly of human experiences: these have been interpreted by the biblical authors in such a way as to disclose religious insights which are of the greatest value. Not all the interpretations we now find appropriate, but the uniqueness of the Bible rests not on particular passages but in the fact that it is possible to discover throughout the whole a growing and developing interpretation of human life in terms of a deepening sensitivity to love, goodness, beauty, moral values and social justice. For Christians these find their fulfilment in the New Testament witness to the life of Jesus. The total impact of the Bible is to hold before men

61

observations of human experience which have been interpreted religiously and disclose a dimension of life of unparalleled importance to which men have given the name God. Many Quakers would I think be willing to accept a similar approach to the scriptures of all the world's great religions.

Signals of transcendence

Having I hope established something of the nature of so-called religious experiences it is now possible to look more closely at the 'signals of transcendence' selected by Peter Berger in his book to which I made reference earlier. As with my brief summary of the points from Alistair Kee's book I trust that I shall give a fair picture, in an extremely condensed form, of Peter Berger's extended argument. As I understand him, he has selected five phenomena that are found within the domain of our natural reality but that appear to point beyond that reality.[39]

Peter Berger first takes man's propensity for order, for mankind continually initiates 'a protective structure of meaning erected in the face of chaos'.[40] His second 'signal of transcendence' is the argument from play. People playing a game deliberately withdraw for a short while from the hard basic facts of life; they set up a man-made universe with its own rules and so for a brief while suspend the rules and assumptions of the serious world. In play, man steps out of one time into another, and thus brackets for a moment the reality that we are 'all living towards death'.

In a somewhat similar but distinct vein, Peter Berger's third signal consists of 'hope' which is another essential element in the human situation. In a world surrounded by death on all sides man continues to be a being who says 'no' to death.

For his fourth signal, Peter Berger uses 'the argument from damnation', which men experience when an event fundamentally outrages their moral sense. Their condemnation of such acts is absolute and certain, and goes beyond this world alone. The fifth and final signal chosen by Peter Berger is that of the argument from humour. We have all been faced with situations so tragic that laughter is the only thing that keeps us sane. For humour implies that the situation is not fixed and will be overcome—it mocks the 'serious' business of the world and the mighty who carry it on.

Peter Berger does not claim that these five signals are the only ones that are pointers to a religious interpretation of the human situation. They do appeal to me as a way in which many people (including at least a part of me) who are unable to go along with a more conventional approach to religion, might yet find through them, and through other signals that will have particular meaning for them, a way of escape from the imprisonment of the prevailing claustrophobic atmosphere of a mechanistic interpretation of life.

Kathleen Bliss has made this point well when she says ' . . . thoughtful men everywhere are seeking for an understanding of the human dimension deep enough and strong enough to stand against those tides in the modern world that threaten man'.[41]

Religion and personality

In any Quaker meeting for worship a great and rich variety of human experience will be available, focussed in the personalities of those attending. The resources of some will possibly be richer than those of others, but each in his own way will have something different and unique to contribute. As I have said earlier each one of us brings to the meeting the gift of himself as a unique and unrepeatable human being. What does this mean? In answering this question I have drawn in the first place on non-Quaker sources to indicate that the approach to religious faith I am making is not just a Quaker quirk but one recognized by other Christians.

Harry Williams, that cheerful monk who writes with such sensitivity on these issues, has truly said, 'men and women should be regarded as persons with their own incalculable character, needs and aspirations . . . for with enormous strength and depth of feeling men and women spend their time searching for their own identity'. What does being a person involve? Harry Williams answers that it means 'being fully alive as body and mind', and he suggests that to be successful in their search for identity people 'have to experience communion with another person at a very deep level—a communion involving for each of them almost all of what they are'. Asked what a person exists to do, Harry Williams replies 'a person exists to be the agent of creative goodness. When we thus create goodness we are both ourselves raised from the dead and also the agents to others for resurrection, for genuine goodness always brings life'.[42]

This dimension of the concept of personality and its relatedness to a religious attitude to life is carried further by a Unitarian, Stephen Spinks when he comments that, 'Today, as in New Testament times, the relationship between individuals is again being recognized as the core of all forms of religious life'.[43]

With the growth of modern biology and its marvellous disclosures of the chemical structure of physical life the scientists concerned have made intricate models of wire and coloured plastic balls to demonstrate the construction of complicated molecules. That for example of DNA, which they use in order to help us laymen understand the biological structure by which life is transmitted. The biologist knows that his model is not a molecule of DNA but gives a fairly accurate image of the truth. It is now popular for theologians to seek for models, that in a similar way will help to convey an image of something of what they mean when they use concepts such as God.

For religious men, including Quakers, human personality can serve as a vivid and powerful model for the concept of God, provided always that like all analogies, it is not pressed too far. For God is not to be thought of as an individual person, as you and I are individuals, but rather as the ground of our being. We have already noted that some Quakers have no difficulty in conceiving God, as he who is the transcendent reality, while others are more diffident, and are only able to take hold of those signals of transcendence which point to a religious interpretation of human life. In either case both groups may be able to see some common ground in the model of human personality, especially in the use of language associated with personal relationships. As John Macquarrie, another Anglican theologian, has said, 'If we use the personal name "God" to denote the other it is because we believe that personal categories do more justice to the notion of our experience than impersonal categories',[44]

The need to love and be loved

Among the rich variety of human experience represented in a Quaker meeting there is certain to be much that relates to human personality, and especially to personalities in relationship and communion with one another. To these complex but most common and natural human relationships, we give the name love. It is exceedingly difficult to think of love in abstract terms, and in fact we do not really know its meaning when expressed in such terms. In a real sense there is no such thing as love, but only loving people, loving thoughts and loving actions. Nevertheless, deep within us we know that we cannot exist as real people unless we are in some degree loved and able to love. This remains true despite the fact that personal relationships are not always easy: sometimes they can be extremely difficult and even bad. But bad relationships high-light the value we place on good ones. We always regret and condemn the bad, and accept and praise the good.

This was vividly brought home to me some years ago in a Juvenile Court of all places. With my fellow magistrates I was hearing a case against a boy charged with perpetrating an ingenious fraud. The proceedings had reached the point where the Clerk of the Court asked the boy's parents what they wished to say about their son. They usually tell us that their child is a paragon of virtue who has been corrupted by the evil boy next door. On this occasion the father stood up and, pointing to his child, announced that he and his wife, shamed by the disgrace the lad had brought on the family, wished to have no more to do with him. They were literally throwing him out of their home. I shall never forget the awful look of abject despair on that boy's face as he heard his father publicly disown and reject him. At that moment he ceased to be a person with any shred of human dignity and became instead a broken lump of de-humanized flesh and bone. The Court took on an hellish atmosphere: the Clerk was the first to recover himself, and asked if there was anyone else who could speak for the boy. A man, sitting at the back of the room said he wished to say something. He was the boy's school teacher and assured us that there was no aspect of his character that had escaped his notice. Despite this, he said that he and his wife believed that there was good in the lad, and they would like to take him into their home as a foster-child, and try to give him the affection, love and security that he so obviously lacked. As he was speaking the transformation in that boy's face was miraculous. Once again he was a real person: for someone loved and cared for him.

The witness of Jesus

This simple, costly act by a man who cared so deeply for another human person, strongly-reinforced for me my overwhelming conviction that love is indeed the truth about life. When we come to meeting we come to acknowledge the worth and value of such love which arises constantly in human experience and continually transcends it. But human love is a fragile thing and although it has within it the seeds of self-giving and self-sacrifice, it can go sour and fail us. It is here that the life of Jesus and the way in which he met his death, powerfully underline our conviction as to the ultimate power and creativeness of love. Quakers have always hesitated to confine their respect and admiration for this particular life, and its self-authenticating authority, in any credal formula or dogmatic definition, for the simple reason that it is too great a manifestation of the human spirit and its potential to be so confined. They are therefore left free to reach their own conclusions about his divinity and status.

Again support for this long held Quaker approach comes from a modern source outside the Society. In *The Future of Religion* Kathleen Bliss has written, 'There never has been *a* way of thinking or feeling about the person of Jesus Christ. Modes of thinking have changed from one age and place to another with cultural background, even if the formal doctrines held among Christians about his person have remained more or less constant. Religious experience has varied too, not only from one age to another but from one person to another: this is now better understood, in the light of psychology, than it ever was before'.[45]

As far as the Society of Friends is concerned its whole witness from the seventeenth century onwards has testified to the tremendous and revolutionary impact that the life of Jesus has made on the Quaker understanding of human experience.

Friends, along with other Christians, have recognized that it was not only the truth, power and simplicity of his teaching that calls for their obedience. In meeting his death with the words of forgiveness on his lips for those who executed him, Jesus disclosed a way of dealing with evil and released into the world a stream of loving and creative energy by which human wickedness can be transmuted. The death of Jesus did not end his contribution to mankind, for all that was of the deepest value in the life of Jesus continues to make its impact on people who are open to the loving spirit in which he lived.

In this sense every Quaker meeting gathers under the shadow of the cross; not the shadow cast by an angry God seeking vengeance and retribution but of the God who is love. For the whole purport of the teaching, life and death of Jesus is his unshaken conviction that God is love. In one sense the execution of Jesus was a human act carried out by a society that did not comprehend his goodness. He was a threat to the established orders of religion and politics and had to be eliminated by them. This terrible human event only makes true sense when it is interpreted from a religious standpoint. Then it discloses the truth that suffering, accepted as Jesus accepted it, can become a source of life and not of destruction. For many Friends this is among the supreme signals for transcendence.

A pattern of life

Throughout all the incidents to which I have made reference in this section it is, I believe, possible to discern a pattern of life and a movement of growth and development characterized by the spirit of love and truth, which links naturally with the discoveries that we can make for ourselves as we take our silent journey to the still centre of our lives. I realize that I have placed considerable emphasis on the importance of personality, more perhaps than some Friends would wish; especially those who feel strong attraction to eastern religions which have as their goal escape from the bonds of earthly life into a realm where individuals lose their personal identity in boundless infinity. I am sure that religions of the west have a great deal to learn from those of the east, especially in their sense of detachment from earthly things. I remain convinced that Quakerism, which grew from Christian roots, will continue to draw its main nourishment from that source, because of its stubborn conviction that life is basically good. What is evil in the world calls for action to redeem and change it, not for the desire to escape from it with all its contingent actualities.

There is one last element that must be included in any answer we try to give as to who or what it is that we worship. I find it relatively easy to convince myself that the cumulative evidence of the religious interpretation of human experience, and the many signals of transcendence that arise from it, all point to a dimension that is beyond and to which one might properly ascribe the name God. This is especially true when I take sensitively into account the continued witness of those Friends, and Christians associated with other churches, together with people of religious faith everywhere, who often seem to have a clearer view about communion with God as the source of all life, power and love. The witness of such people is only effective when it is demonstrated in the quality of their lives.

I know that my atheist friends tell me that there is no point in asking questions about the origin of the universe and life, as there can be no answer to them, nevertheless these questions will not let me go. While I recognize that I am not being very logical, I still feel strongly drawn at this level of my experience in what may seem a rather detached manner to opt for belief in God. The illogicality of my position was brought home to me

by reflection on the words of a humanist who addressed a
large group of Friends about the nature of his convictions. He
defined his outlook in some such words as these. 'Before birth
there is nothing: after death there is nothing: but between
birth and death it is possible to impose on life some degree of
order that will make for the greater happiness of man.' Provided I could substitute 'to create love' for his phrase 'to
impose order', I found myself able to go along with him but
with one major exception. I felt constrained to go one vital step
further. In so attempting to create love in life I felt in the
depths of my being that I was responding to something that
was already there. Perhaps this reflects the cosmic reference in
Dante's mind when he wrote in *Paradiso*, 'The love that moves
the sun and the other stars'.

The leadings of God

What is the connection between this desire to respond to
something that is given in life coupled with the powerful sense
I have of values that transcend everyday human experience and
can be interpreted as religious experience, and the concept of
God as the source of all that is? I find the convincing link in the
understanding of the experience of stillness in the depth of my
being, and I am sure this is true for other Friends.

In all my thinking about belief in God I recognize the
powerful impression made upon me in 1939 by John Baillie's
book *Our Knowledge of God*. I found his phrase 'mediated
immediacy' specially illuminating. John Baillie argued that men
have no direct awareness of the presence of God that is
mediated to them apart from their experience of the world.

This approach made sense of the teaching given to me
throughout my childhood when my parents spoke as if God
was immediately and obviously present—yet to me he did not

seem to be so. It also made sense of the Quaker conviction that men have direct access to God.

The point at issue becomes clear when one thinks about the question of guidance. I would hesitate to claim that I receive direct guidance from God—I do not hear a divine voice that tells me what to do. But I do have a sense that I am being drawn to take one course of action rather than another. The guidance, however, arises from a countless number of experiences, influences, attitudes and disciplines which I have accumulated over the years and upon which I have reflected. So certain types of action seem to be my natural response to particular circumstances. In them all the sense of the presence of God is real and immediate but it is not unmediated.

The Holy Spirit

It may have surprised some Friends, and alarmed others, that so far in this section I have made no reference to the Holy Spirit. Surely, they will say, the doctrine of the spirit is that part of structured Christianity that has the greatest appeal to Quakers. I am sure that this is true. I must confess that the notion of the spirit of God interpenetrating the spirit of man an exceedingly difficult one to grasp as it has been traditionally expressed. I once confessed my difficulty to a Friend who said 'But surely the Holy Spirit has tapped you on the shoulder'. 'No,' I said, 'he has never done so.' 'But,' he replied, 'you have fallen in love!' Well yes! If that is what is meant, then I do know the action of the spirit, but I would have to say that it was a religious interpretation of a normal and natural human experience.

Yet I am aware that for many Quakers this sense of the powerful prompting of the spirit in their lives is of overwhelming importance. In its *Advices* the Society calls its members to 'Take heed, dear Friends, to the promptings of love and truth in your hearts, which are the leadings of God . . . ', pointing out that as disciples of Jesus, 'we are called to live in the life and power of the Holy Spirit'.[46] I can accept this advice addressed to me as a member of the Religious Society of Friends. But I would have difficulty in telling people who have no religious frame of reference (and most of our contemporaries do not) that I was living in the life and power of the Holy Spirit. They would rightly want to know what was meant by the phrase. Their question would challenge me to think what these words mean to me. My understanding of them is finely expressed by Harry Williams when he writes 'The spirit is ourselves in the depths of what we are. It is me at the profoundest level of my being the level at which I can no longer distinguish between what is myself and what is greater than me. So, theologically, the Spirit is called God in me . . . the place where God and me mingle indistinguishably'.[47]

We come back once again to the deep still place at the centre of our being, where we are alone, and yet not alone, for we are compassed about and caught up in so great a cloud of witnesses. It is the most human of all human experiences, and at the same time the experience that cries aloud for a religious interpretation. Today, and throughout its history, the Society of Friends has felt constrained to interpret this experience, always with flexibility and freedom, as an encounter with the spirit of love, and truth and light, for which the only adequate name available is the name God. We did not drag God in—he was there all the time.

IV

MAKING THE BEST USE OF QUAKER WORSHIP

People coming freshly to a Quaker meeting frequently ask,
'are there techniques of Quaker worship that I can learn in
order to be able to practise the Quaker method more effectively'? When I have to answer such a question I always find
myself getting hung up on the word technique. To me, it
implies that one can set about Quaker worship in a manner
similar to that in which a musician follows a certain method of
procedure concerned with the practical details, disciplines and
formal skills in playing his instrument. Quaker worship just
doesn't seem to be like that. At the same time I realize that my
questioner is most likely, nowadays, to have in mind the
practices associated with such activities as transcendental
meditation, or, if he is an older person, with the traditional
disciplines involved in more classical religious exercises such
as prayer, meditation or contemplation.

So if my questioner is asking, 'Is there a particular method of
Quaker worship which everyone can learn and should follow'?
my answer would have to be a straight no. If, on the other
hand, he is asking, 'Are there some techniques, in the sense of a
variety of procedures, disciplines and practices, which may
help one to make the most effective use of a Quaker meeting,
then I would answer yes in a general kind of way. Indeed from
the way in which I have written about a typical meeting and the
role that silent waiting plays in it, I hope I have made it
abundantly plain that Quaker worship, though not without
shape and form, is, by its very nature, spontaneous and

extremely flexible. It does not lend itself to pre-ordained patterns for it must provide for variety and growth.

This point can be illustrated by the inquiry of a BBC producer, seeking to make the best distribution of microphones in a studio from which a Quaker meeting was to be broadcast. 'Which of these people will speak?' he asked. He was told that it was not possible to say who, if anyone, might have anything to say. It was clear from the look of alarm and surprise with which he greeted this reply, that he had obviously not come across a way of worship that allowed for such freedom.

With heart and mind prepared

The Society of Friends has been most sensitive to the dynamic, living, organic form of a Quaker meeting, and has therefore not attempted to lay down rules as to how it should be conducted. It has, however, addressed *Advices and queries* to its members, and one of these will make an excellent basis for our consideration of ways by which it is possible to make the best use of Quaker worship. It simply advises Friends to come to meeting 'with hearts and minds prepared'. This of course, does not mean 'don't come if neither your emotions nor your thoughts seem to be in a proper state of readiness for the activity of worship'. It could well be that, when you least feel like it, that is the very time when you most need to go.

No, the advice given, backed by a long history of experience, is suggesting that some kind of preparation during the week will give you the best chance of getting the most out of Quaker worship, as well as enabling you to give the most you can to it. In the earlier sections of this book I have said that in meeting itself people will discover for themselves ways in which they can most naturally enter its life. Exactly the same principle applies to methods of preparation for worship, but it is obviously sensible to see what guide-lines the Society suggests for setting about the preparation of heart and mind. A strong hint is given (and this I have already referred to on page 24) that some time should be set aside, each day, for a period of inward retirement: a quaint phrase much loved by Quakers of an earlier generation. Fortunately the Society offers its advice in the most general terms and leaves it to Friends to decide, what is the best time of the day for them to use for a period of quiet.

There are many Friends who clearly find that the early morning is most suitable, while others prefer a later time. A similar freedom is suggested for the way in which the time should be used. The quiet period can include the reading of the Bible, or other religious writings and devotional books, as well as reflection upon them. The practice of prayer is encouraged, and to this, with the related subjects of meditation and contemplation, I shall give attention later in this section.

At this point I must refer my readers back to the section of this book dealing with the role of silence, where, in particular, I remarked on the two-fold purpose of a time of inward retirement. The first being the personal re-enforcement of one's own grasp of religious insights and values; the second, the actual self-preparation for the corporate activity of silent worship. Again, as in the case of attempting to describe Quaker worship the solution would be in the achievement of one, immediate expression of everything that needs to be said. Because this is not possible the various elements involved have to be dealt with one by one.

Four preliminary remarks must be made. First, there is no perfect order in which this analysis can be carried out. I have therefore chosen one that appeals to me, but I fully realize that other Friends would deal with the issues in a different order. Second, whatever private spiritual disciplines we follow for the sustenance of our interior life, they are inextricably intertwined with our actual preparation for worship, and mutually react on each other. Third, we must never consider preparation for worship as the occasion for the deliberate preparation of something we are determined to say in meeting. I shall deal with this point more fully in the following section. Fourth, we must keep constantly in mind that the provision we make for times of quiet reflection, including their duration and their content, will vary greatly from person to person, and vary, too, for people themselves at different times of their lives.

A structured approach

As I propose to start by describing, what might be called a more structured approach; I must say now that this is not the kind that I, personally, find of the greatest help. From my Anglican days, which embraced close association with the low church evangelicals and the middle of the road position, as well as with the high church anglo-catholic tradition, I was made to feel constantly guilty by the practical assumption, although there seemed no actual authority for it, that a quiet time in the morning was evidence of greater piety than of one at any other time of the day. It so happens that I am not at my brightest in the early morning, and all my attempts to carry out any sort of spiritual exercises at that time of the day, only resulted in my falling off to sleep again. During those periods when I did achieve some kind of regular quiet time they did not produce the kind of constructive results that others discovered and that only made me feel more guilty. These experiences convinced me that we must be extremely honest and gentle with ourselves as to what kind of inward retirement is the most appropriate for us, even if to some it is virtually unrecognizable as such. While not seeking to impose our way upon others, we can ask them to be equally sensitive in their attitude to ours.

However we approach our withdrawal from our normal preoccupation with the necessary business and activities of our lives, it would seem important that the time of disinvolvement should include a period of silence. This will enable us to make the journey to the inner side of ourselves and the rediscovery of the still centre. What I have already said about the variety of ways in which this interior journey can, and is, approached in meeting for worship, applies equally to that made in our private opportunities. As most of us find it far from easy to switch off abruptly the currents of thought flowing through our minds it will probably be helpful to concentrate our attention upon some particular object.

As I have mentioned, the Society encourages its members to read the Bible daily, although I would guess that the number of Friends who actually do so is relatively small. Its use, or that of other similar literature, is especially appropriate as an introduction to a period of private meditation. The deliberate reading of such writings may well be the means that will help us to enter into a dimension in which the religious purposes of life are given paramount importance. But the reading should be carried out in a manner in which criticism of the text is subordinate to attempts to discover how the passage is, in fact, a religious interpretation of the ordinary human experience which is the basis of its content. The focus we desire may well be achieved by the reading of a mere sentence or so, which will divert our attention from our active thoughts so that we can concentrate upon the real significance of the meaning of the words, and begin our deeper reflection.

While I have made particular mention of the Bible and similar writings, I recognize that the focussing of attention can be achieved by any number of means. Many Friends, for example, find the reading of poetry or devotional anthologies of great value: some will be able to dispense with printed sources and rely upon their stored memories, as the point of their departure towards the interior.

Reflection on life

No programme can be set out as to the exact nature of the inward exploration but some likely features of it can be noted. Plato's comment that the unexamined life is not worth living is relevant here, because in our search, we shall no doubt reflect upon the quality of our lives, attempting to view them in the light of values to which we are committed. We should not be afraid to be thankful for those things in us that come near to matching the quality of human life displayed in Jesus. The journey towards the centre is not intended to be a grim effort of relentless introspection which discovers only the evil in us: but rather one of joyful acceptance of the things that are good, beautiful and true.

At the same time, if our search is an honest one, we shall inevitably discover much in our experience that falls far short of the human potential expressed in the life of Jesus. Traditionally this awareness of self-centredness and sense of falling short of the ideals we most admire, had been called sin, a word not greatly favoured today for a variety of reasons. Two in particular seem important. The popular use of the word fails to take adequately into account the determinist pressures that arise from our normal human appetites, which are part of our psychological make-up. The word also implies a state of human imperfection which is abhorrent to a Holy God, and inevitably separates us from him. One of the splendid insights coming to us from seventeenth-century Quakerism is expressed thus by William Penn. 'The Light of Christ within, who is the Light of the World, and so a light to you that tells you the truth of your condition, leads all that take heed unto it out of darkness into God's marvellous light; for light grows upon the obedient . . . Wherefore, O friends, turn in, turn in, I beseech you. Where is the poison, there is the antidote; there you want Christ and there you must find Him—and, blessed be God, there you may find Him.'[48]

The fact William Penn is stating is that though we may discover darkness within, we can also discover within the antidote to its poison, in the light. In modern terms this means that we can accept and forgive ourselves because of our conviction that love is the truth about life. Loving implies the willingness to forgive, and God is love. Another feature of our inward journey is certain to be heightened perception of the nature of our relationships with other people. We may need to try to forgive and accept them, or to make some special attempt to understand their attitudes to us or ours to them.

The important principles underlying the contents of the foregoing paragraphs were powerfully expressed in a brave and sensitive letter to *The Friend* of 23 February 1973. Anne Wilson wrote: ' . . . Before I was rescued by psycho-analysis, my problem was that I admitted guilt the whole time, condemning and punishing myself for quite natural human failings. I thought only perfection was acceptable. The result was a continuous and agonizing anxiety, and a considerable amount of physical illness, due to the resulting tension. This syndrome is common, in varying degrees of severity. The world is full of people who are haunted by unjustified guilt because they cannot accept their own natures and therefore fear the harm their "wickedness" may do. I often wonder what Christianity, as it is understood by us poor weak beings who understand human nature so little, has to say to such people. It was my psychiatrist who showed me that only those who can love themselves are able to love others, and that only those who can be self-forgiving can be all-forgiving. People who are self-condemning are likely to be envious and therefore to wish people ill.

79

We cannot love our neighbours by order. If we can feel a loving kindness towards ourselves, and therefore spontaneously love others, we shall spontaneously feel remorse when we harm them and wish to make reparation.

Would we not be wiser if we were to stop asking too much of ourselves and instead decide to recognize and accept the complexities and ambivalence in our natures? With this recognition can come an understanding and loving kindness which gives new insights into concepts such as judgement, self-discipline, guilt, repentance, change and responsibility.'

So far I have written of what might be described as the personal aspect of our journey inwards. But there is another aspect which we cannot avoid. Friends have taken to heart the prayer of John Wilhem Rowntree, '. . . lay on us the burden of the world's suffering'. As modern people we are only too painfully conscious of it, and aware that we cannot see a way through the complexities of human situations. Because of their magnitude, contemplation of such situations could easily cause us to give up trying to change things, or to harden ourselves, so that their pain did not reach us. The journey inward serves to keep us sensitive so that we do what we can, while enabling us to recognize that we are not expected to carry the whole crushing weight.

Prayer

Christians have traditionally used the word 'prayer' to cover both our dealings with ourselves, and also our dealings with others, for it was the process by which we communicated with God, on our own behalf and also on behalf of other people. It has become, for modern people, a loaded word, which is difficult for them to use for it is completely without meaning. This is largely because it implies a personal approach to God, which smacks of auto-suggestion, for to many people God is merely a projection of man's deep unconscious desires. Even for those to whom God is a reality, prayer seems so often an attempt to appeal to him to deal mercifully with us, or others, in a manner that would require a suspension of natural law. So prayer appears to be an attempt to manipulate God who, if not a projection, is at best a remote distant being to whom when we are in difficulty it is comforting to address a cry of help.

When I think back to my childhood and the teaching I was given about prayer, I realize that it is not surprising that such strange ideas about prayer are firmly rooted in us. There was, for example, an occasion when, having assembled my model railway, I found myself utterly frustrated, simply because I could not make the clockwork engine function as I had mislaid the key. With mounting agitation I searched frantically for it, then with childlike trust, I knelt down by my tracks asking God to show me where the key was. In those few moments while I was calm, I remembered where the key was kept; I saw it in my mind's eye lying in a drawer. Immediately I rose from my knees, went to the drawer and there, sure enough, was the key. This incident convinced me that there was a secret power in prayer, and I felt that I had discovered an infallible way of achieving a particular desire that at that time dominated my mind. I desperately wanted Oxford to beat Cambridge in the forthcoming University boat race. Despite the diligence with which I commended Oxford's cause to the Lord they were hopelessly beaten!

Thereafter prayer seemed virtually a ritual required of Christians, not however likely to be very effective, but too risky to drop entirely! As I grew up, I gradually recognized how childish and magical my attitude to prayer was. I tried to change it without much success, yet I continued to pray, for the requirement had been strongly instilled in me, but little by little the activity lost what meaning it had. This caused me embarrassment, because I was obviously not functioning properly as a Christian. Finally I gave up the practice of formal prayer altogether, and then, of course felt more guilty than ever.

When I first became associated with the Society of Friends my interest in prayer as a meaningful possibility for adult people was revived. This was largely because so many of the Quakers I knew displayed such a positive attitude to life. Their personalities and characters revealed an integrity, power and security to which their practice of prayer clearly contributed. For them prayer was a joyful, natural thing: the possession of the riches of their interior lives. They spoke of it as the means by which they held a regular simple communion with a loving God, which coloured their lives with tranquillity. I was particularly struck by the fact that those of them who seemed most sincere, real people were reluctant to use the word prayer too easily. At the time that I was going to my tribunal as a conscientious objector, and specially needed their support they said they would 'think of me'. Whereas most other Christians would have offered to 'pray for me'. I knew that the thinking of my Quaker friends would be a deeply sincere imaginative, involved activity based upon their loving concern for me as a person, and coupled with their real experience of a loving purpose arising within but transcending normal life.

It was through another incident, again concerned with children, that I came to see fully that there was an entirely different manner of looking at prayer. When my children were small, I adopted the habit of looking in on them last thing at night before retiring to bed. The sight of them sleeping so peacefully, yet so vulnerable, drew from the depths of my being the unspoken longing that I should adequately fulfil my parental responsibilities towards them, coupled with a strong sense of commitment to this vision of fatherhood, so that they might grow up in an atmosphere of loving security.

Prayer as passionate thinking

Slowly I came to realize that this silent activity of mine was something very near to a meaning of prayer that could be real for me. It was a perfectly ordinary human experience which also had a transcendent quality about it, and was open to a religious interpretation. Praying in this sense is a natural response on our part and cannot be separated from our journey inwards. That journey is our prayer, our resting in and responding to the loving meaning of life. It well may be that, during our time of inward retirement, we shall want to think of someone in particular who needs reassurance or support. We then turn our attention to them, trying to imagine their situation, and letting our deep desire for their well-being fill our thought. 'Prayer,' says John Macquarrie, 'is a fundamental style of thinking, passionate and compassionate, responsive and thankful, that is deeply rooted in our humanity and that manifests itself not only among believers but also among serious-minded people who do not profess any religious faith'.[49]

When we pray for someone or for the members of our meeting by way of compassionate thinking, we accept an obligation to try, as far as we can, to answer our own prayer by some action for the person or persons on whose behalf we have prayed. If such direct action is not possible, then we should see how we can be the agent for loving and imaginative goodness for a person who is within our range.

We must be as frank as we can over this business of loving, accepting and forgiving another person. While I am absolutely convinced that this is what we must strive for, I am equally convinced that it is one of the hardest things we are called upon to do. However hard we try we shall find, all too frequently, that we fail. Sometimes when we are really honest we shall be able to admit that the grudge we hold against someone, because of some disservice, or outright nastiness they have perpetrated against us, is not one that we even want to relinquish.

Even those who strongly interpret their experience as a direct communion with God, and therefore feel able to seek his help in enabling them to achieve the act of reconciliation, willingly admit that it is not an easy activity. Some of them betray by their attitudes and behaviour that they have not, in fact, forgiven the injury despite the pious language they use to convince us that they have! I, who am much more hesitant to speak of prayer in anything approaching conventional terms, know from sad, personal experience how difficult it is to accept and forgive someone who has wounded my pride by striking at my self-esteem. So I feel quite unable to pontificate on this state of affairs. All I can do is to make three quite undogmatic comments arising from my experience.

First, harbouring a grudge against life in general, or a particular circumstance or person brings about a bitter, unhealthy state in our personality and tends to diminish us as a person. Second, the fact that we recognize this is, at least, one positive sign that we are moving in the right direction. Third, one thing I have found helpful is to try to avoid a hasty confrontation with the person concerned as this can so often lead to hurtful unconstructive recriminations, when we say things we later bitterly regret. At the same time I am fully aware of the damage done by bottling up one's outraged feelings, quite apart from the fact that the unwillingness to tell people when they have hurt us indicates a lack of integrity which is destructive of real human relations. Of course, there are people, so loving and perfectly in control of themselves, that they can handle positions of direct confrontation with delicacy and constructiveness. But they are rare people, and many who feel they can act in this way have, so frequently, in my experience deluded themselves that I feel they should consider their position with the greatest care.

Overcoming aggression

My way of overcoming this aspect of the problem is to keep a sort of 'journal of hate', in which, when necessary, I write out as fully and vividly as possible exactly what I think of the offending person, and the details of his hateful action as I see them, together with the way in which he has so blatantly misunderstood my good intentions. In so writing, I find first of all, an outlet for my aggressive feelings. Also, much against my current desires, a sense of fairness creeps in as I seek to describe my opponent's case. Little by little I begin to see the situation in a better, more balanced perspective. There will, of course, be occasions when some immediate action to redress the situation is called for, but whenever possible I would still prefer to deal with the position by way of writing. Only this time it will take the form of a letter to the offender, but written with the strict proviso on my part, that it is not to be dispatched until at least I have had the chance of sleeping on it. With the reflection gained by a few hours delay I have rarely sent anything like the original draft, or even anything at all. Because I find that on re-reading what I have written while filled with the burning sense of the justice of my cause and the righteous indignation of my immediate reactions, I have inevitably over-stated my case. This has helped me to become more able to state my view with the moderation that comes from my sense that I too shared considerable responsibility for the misunderstanding.

Whatever form my writing actually takes, it usually results in the ability to discuss the situation, coolly and calmly, with my adversary; a conversation which may well pave the way to a better understanding and ultimate reconciliation. Dealing with our inner, or outer, conflicts is an aspect of our lives to which we need to respond with the greatest patience, and to recognize that it may be years before we are finally able to give up a grudge, and accept and forgive the person who caused it. This is even harder when the person in question has not actually done anything particularly nasty to us. It's just that his attitudes and approach to life simply irritate us, probably as the result of a clash of temperaments. We should always remember that we are asked to love people and not necessarily to like them. In the same sense we have to learn to love ourselves by a willingness to accept ourselves as just ordinary people, prone to failings that we do not particularly like or admire. One final advantage of keeping a 'bad temper' journal, is the source of amusement and instruction that it will afford us, when, years later we look back on the account we have written of some incident that at the time caused us such bitter agony. When I do this, I am filled with amazement that I could have got into such a state over such trivial events—trivial only when seen with hindsight!

Many people can achieve a sense of proportion that is the first step on the road to reconciliation without the exercise of writing. The kind of exercise that is so delightfully reflected in Don Camillo's self conversations before the Crucifix, about his running battle, as the Priest of a small Italian town, with its Communist Mayor, exactly illustrates my point. In fact, to achieve a quality coming anywhere near that of traditional prayer for religious people, all such dialogues, whether silent, talking to oneself, or to a trusted friend, or writing must be conducted in the light of our signals of transcendence. These disciplines certainly can assist us greatly when we engage in the act of disinvolvement from the ordinary activity of life, and are as valid forms of prayer as any that have been used by our more conventional religious ancestors. This kind of discipline practised with diligence also helps us to behave in a more truly

Christian-religious manner when we are called upon to deal with a situation that brooks no delay.

Meditation

Just as in the silence of corporate Quaker worship we are drawn deeper and deeper towards the still centre, so in our private worship we find our thoughts give place to a deep silence of the mind. The steps by which this is achieved have, in classic Christianity, been described first as meditation, defined by John Macquarrie as '. . . letting the mind become immersed in the concepts, symbols, teachings, dogmas, stories of the Christian faith'.[50] This statement expands a Quaker one by Thomas F. Green, who, in his Swarthmore Lecture described meditation as 'a centring of thought on a definite religious subject'.[51] Our Swiss Friend, Pierre Lacout, who has written so lucidly on the subject of the discipline of inner silence in *God is Silence*, carries us forward to the second step, that of contemplation. For he writes 'contemplative silence is a way of seeing which needs no object. It can only be defined as direction. It is a looking towards, not a looking at. Ideas about God are good only if I move quickly on from them'.[52] The goal of our private worship, into which we draw the friends for whom we have prayed, is the deep still centre at the core of our being. It is here we fulfil the intention of Peter Berger's words 'the fundamental religious impulse is not to theorize about transcendence but to worship it'.[53]

Certainly many Friends have found the practice of meditation, some of it strongly Christo-centric, some highly flavoured with eastern ideas, to be a help rather than a hindrance in their approach to private and public worship. Also many modern Quakers who have written about worship, have emphasized the value of relaxation of the body and with it the control of breathing. I have been interested to learn from many Friends how, in particular, they have found the exercises associated with Yoga, whether or not they follow its full philosophy, to constitute for them a vital part of the way in which they follow the Society's advice to engage in a regular time of inward retirement.

In certain parts of America I have noticed that a few Friends have adopted the lotus position of sitting in meeting. It was in that country, too, that I had the opportunity of talking with a number of young Quakers who, twice a day, undertook a private meditation discipline. This they began by adopting a lotus position as the one most likely to promote the total relaxation of every muscle, which was further achieved by concentrating upon each one in turn. The next step in the process was the exhalation of breath from the lungs by the contraction of the diaphragm, followed by the slow intake of air in rhythmic breathing.

The continuous repetition of the 'mantra'—a particular word private to each person, or the similar use of a phrase, helped them to lose themselves—for the object of their act of meditation was to achieve an emptiness of mind. They admitted it was not easy to get rid of thoughts, but in those brief moments when this state was reached they would say they had a 'god experience', although they would prefer not to use the word, but to think of the experience as one in which they had 'tapped' the source of energy at the centre of all life. The result of their meditation was that they were made calm, and felt refreshed and filled with energy.

They were clear, however, that valuable as this meditation was for their private purposes, it was not the kind of meditation they would wish to adopt in a Quaker meeting, for then they wanted to be open to people and engage in a form of meditation that was corporate, and I entirely agree with them.

An unstructured approach

Pierre Lacout, in the booklet to which I have made reference, makes the point that if we are to be spiritually aware, 'we must make up our minds, clearly and deliberately to set aside every day a certain period of time for this life'.[54] I have given considerable space to the way in which such a regular time could be used because I am well aware that, for many Friends, this is a discipline that they gladly impose upon themselves because of the need that it meets in them for the strengthening of their spiritual selves. Earlier in this section (p. 76) I indicated that I personally do not find such an ordered, disciplined approach helpful, although I recognize its validity and obvious value to those who practise it. I have good reason to believe that I am not alone in this, for there are a large number of Friends who have told me that their response to the Society's advice is no longer along traditional lines. The approach we make we feel is in line with the widely held Quaker view, that the whole of life is a preparation for worship. It is widely held, because it applies equally to those Friends who do deliberately set aside a daily period of time for the cultivation of spiritual values, as well as by those of us who follow a less disciplined approach.

There is one obvious danger that must be faced immediately by those who claim that the whole of life is a preparation for worship; it is that life can slip by so easily, almost unnoticed, and we drift into a position where no concrete steps are taken or active preparation is in fact made. But it was the recognition of the way that, in my own case, my more diffuse approach had grown quietly in my experience, that caused me to see its effectiveness for me. It seems to fit in with the Quaker sense that no strong line should be drawn between so called sacred things and those labelled secular. It also falls in with the suggestion about the nature of religious experience that I have emphasized so strongly in this book, namely that such experience is the ordinary everyday events of life, carefully observed and interpreted in a religious manner, and seen as signals of transcendence. This attitude does, of course, involve a certain discipline of the observation of experience, which arises from training oneself to look continually at the world in a particular kind of way. There will also be occasions when one takes time consciously to reflect upon experience and to give attention to an interpretative exercise: but they are not set times.

Life as a preparation for worship

In all honesty, therefore, I must confess that I have unconsciously developed a pattern which is akin to the practice of inward retirement, although I would find it hard to see that it has been carried out in any regular or disciplined manner. It is true that for many years, and perhaps in some way all my life, I have been fascinated and excited by efforts to understand life's meaning. This inquisitiveness has found expression, for me, in a great variety of ways, few of which I have felt to be specially religious at the time. Because, as a boy and young man, I was inclined to be shy, and lacked self-confidence, some hidden need urged me to seek to overcome this by consciously trying to make friendships. In the first place this was in order to fulfil my need, but gradually I adopted the practice because of the discovery of the mutual release and enlargement of personality that was incidental to personal relationships. This joy in friendship has been an abiding delight, and has also disclosed the dimension of transcendence. For it encouraged me to try to discover what made people tick; the things that motivated them; the interests they had and especially their views (or non-views) on religion, and their attitudes to life. I was equally interested in the books they read, the films, theatres, TV programmes and music that gripped them. Coupled with similar interests of my own I was, on looking back, storing up a wealth of human experience. Upon this I found that I was continuously reflecting, so that I have over the years in fact devoted a considerable amount of time to this activity, and I suspect this is true of other Friends.

Reading, too, has been a source of great enjoyment and has included a wide variety of books, ranging from modern novels to biographies and even theology (an unusual taste for a Quaker). Devotional books I do not find helpful, and although I was brought up on the practice of reading a Bible portion each day, I have long discontinued this practice, substituting for it the reading of a particular section or whole book to which I have felt drawn. The same attitude guides my reading of Quaker literature such as *Christian Faith and Practice*. Because loving relationships are such an important part of my life I frequently find myself thinking about my friends and acquaintances. This often prompts me to write letters to them as part of the way in which a friendship is sustained. At least in one way it seems, for me, to be what I would consider to be prayerful thought for them. I do not recall adopting any of these activities as a conscious effort at inward retirement, for they arose naturally in the ordinary course of living. It is true that there are frequently times when I wish to turn my mind to some special issue, or to give concentrated attention to the joys or needs of a particular person. More often than not, I find this easier to do by going for a walk. In this I can claim a precedent in George Fox who tells us he 'often walked solitary in Barnet Chase to wait upon the Lord'.[55]

I have written of my experience (but have not attempted to include that of other Friends who follow this more open approach to preparation for worship) because I am convinced that there are many members in the Society, and also newcomers, who fail to recognize that the pattern that has grown naturally within their experience is a valid way of sustaining their personal sense of religious values and of preparing themselves for worship. In fact, the more structured, ordered method and the more open approach have much in common, and it is not unknown for people to use one or other of these methods at various times of their lives.

Quakers and mysticism

I suspect that most Quakers would be inclined to say that the Society falls broadly into the category of mystical religious groups. A number of Friends have attempted to define what this could mean. Rufus M. Jones concludes the Introduction to his *Studies in Mystical Religion* by stating that, 'the Society of Friends is a religious body which has made a serious attempt to unite inward mystical religion with active, social endeavours'.[56] His fellow American Quaker, Howard Brinton, in defining the word writes ' . . . mysticism means direct first-hand experience of the Divine, an actual experience comparable to that in which science is based'. He goes on to quote Dean Inge's comment that ' . . . the Society of Friends is the most mystical sect in Christendom'.[57] In his pamphlet *The Quaker Meeting*, Howard E. Collier emphasizes that 'the mystical experience is the mark of a healthy, uninhibited character: it is not a morbid state'.[58] This point is carried further by Pierre Lacout, from whose essay I have already quoted. He writes that, 'For some "mystic" is synonymous with 'exceptional', involving visions, transports, levitations . . . This is putting the important thing into second place, pushing the central to the periphery. For Paul, a mystic is a person who knows the fullness of Christ, who lives by the inflowing of the Holy Spirit'.[59]

It is significant, however, that the Society of Friends itself has tended to treat mysticism, and mystical experience, with great caution. In fact no direct reference is made to the subject in the index of *Christian Faith and Practice*. This cautious approach receives considerable support from modern Christian sources. 'Mysticism,' says Peter Berger, 'broadly speaking is any religious practice or doctrine that asserts the ultimate unity of man and the divine.' He adds 'mystical religion therefore always looks for salvation within the putative depths of human consciousness itself', which he notes is 'diametrically opposed to the biblical conception of God as one standing outside and against man'.[60] He also notes a severe limitation of 'mystical or any other alleged experiences of the supernatural' as not being available to everyone.

John Macmurray clarifies the position when he writes 'The mystical experience is a very real one, and very fundamental . . . yet in itself the mystic's experience is not knowledge, but rather a vision of what there is to be known. The vision itself is conditioned in many ways by the special influences, the traditions of thought and activity, the institutions and habits which press continuously upon the mystic's life and mould his consciousness'. He adds, 'if the vision is to issue in knowledge it must find expression and definition in thought and language'.[61] A similar point is made by Kathleen Bliss, 'The mystic's first-hand experience of the divine, granting it to be that, becomes a human communication immediately anything is said about it'.[62]

Alistair Kee presents a brief but useful summary of two general types of mystical experience. One of these concerns a new way of seeing the external world, while the other involves a complete and utter withdrawal from the world. He states that 'the mystical experience must be a truly remarkable experience . . . whether occurring spontaneously or being induced either by spiritual exercises or by the use of drugs'.[63] For him, however, the important question is whether mysticism can be accepted as witness to the being of God. His answer is in the negative, as he quotes with approval W. T. Stace, ' . . . the concept of God is an interpretation of the experience, not part of the experience itself'.[64]

These comments of notable Christian thinkers, while underwriting the corporate judgement of the Society of Friends in not placing its absolute reliance on mystical experience as the basis of its life, hardly do justice to the intuitive leanings of many Quakers towards a mystical interpretation of religious faith, whether specifically Christian or not. Perhaps the position of many Friends is neatly summed up in Solzhenitsyn's description of one of his characters in his novel *August 1914*. He says of her, 'she felt that certain concepts of eastern religion were a beautiful complement to Christian beliefs. Her mind did not regard the mixture of the two as in any way contradictory; they were merely alternative manifestations of beauty'.[65]

Individual and corporate worship

So far in this section there has been a considerable overlap between what are helpful attitudes in one's solitary practice of the journey to the interior, and that same journey carried out with and in the company of others. It is not always easy to divide the two, but difficult though it is, I am convinced that some distinctions can and must be made.

The first is that to be of value corporate worship must be held at regular and agreed times. I, who do not care for set periods for private devotion, am quite clear that, from a purely practical point of view, corporate worship by its very nature requires the acceptance, by all who wish to participate, to gather at a particular time, on a particular day in a particular place. As an obvious corollary I would add the importance for everyone to try to be both punctual and regular in their attendance. Points long stressed by the Society for the benefit of the whole worshipping group.

Secondly, whatever the point of departure for our meditation or journey to the inner side of our lives, our intention must be that it should be a corporate exercise—a lending of our minds to one another.

Thirdly, bodily relaxation most certainly has its place, but the extent to which it is practised must be held in balance with the convenience of others present. To take an extreme example: if we find that lying flat on our backs or standing on our heads (both positions I understand form part of Yoga exercises) promote relaxation, these are postures suitable to our solitariness but not when we assemble for public worship.

My fourth point relates to the private reading of books (as distinct from public reading as a contribution to ministry) in meeting. Once again I can illustrate what I have in mind by an extreme case. I recall attending a meeting over a particular period of time, when several Friends present, had no sooner taken their places than they started reading books (most suitable ones that they had brought with them) and continued to do so. After a time, a non-reading Friend rose to speak, whereupon the readers stuck their thumbs in their books to mark their places. Immediately the spoken contribution was ended, the readers removed their thumbs, and continued to read. That meeting never became a gathered one—how could it? For the majority of the worshippers were only concerned with their private thoughts stimulated by their reading, and were clearly making no attempt to share in the life of the meeting with their fellows. This is not to say, that from time to time, an individual worshipper may not find it helpful to read privately a brief passage, in order to re-collect his attention, so that he may the more effectively share in the communion of the meeting. Earlier in this section I have mentioned the personal help I gain through writing—but such an exercise would, I consider, be entirely out of place in meeting.

Pierre Lacout makes the point I am reaching after and links it with my earlier one about the intention of gatheredness with which we should approach our worship. He writes, 'the silence of religious experience is never a silence in which the soul shuts itself up in isolation. It is a silence which opens out on to the infinite in a true communion of minds and hearts, in a real unity founded on respect for diversity . . . a soul gathered in silent worship is never alone with God. It is always in communion with the soul of all other worshippers: its silence plunges it into that inward light which lightens everyman'.[66]

My fifth and final point of distinction between what is suitable in our private devotion but needs modification in our public worship, relates to prayer. Privately, we may concentrate our special attention upon the needs of a particular person or indeed upon our own, thinking with passion and compassion about them. It will also be natural for us to do this in meeting for worship, but with a subtle and important difference in attitude. In meeting we shall silently seek to hold our loved one, or ourselves, in the growing life of the meeting. I must confess to feeling a slight sense of irritation when people speak of Quaker meetings as being 'a time of prayer', because they usually seem to me to mean by this that each Friend is individually seeking some private communication with God, rather than whole-heartedly joining with others in an act of corporate communion.

Corporate contemplation

This prompts me to comment on a remark made, many years ago, by Evelyn Underhill, in her book *Worship*. In dealing with Quaker worship she says 'it is significant that the Society of Friends, the only Christian communion which has made contemplative prayer the standard of worship, has produced no great contemplative or made any real addition to our knowledge of the soul's interior life'.[67]

It never has been and is not now the aim of the Society of Friends to produce outstanding leaders in any particular sphere of the life of the spirit. Its remarkable achievement is for over 300 years to have maintained a form of worship in which people, at any level of spiritual progress, can join in an act of corporate and silent contemplation, and worship of transcendence, to which, if the worshipper feels able, he may rightly give the name of God.

In this section I have tried to indicate some of the ways in which anyone who attends a Quaker meeting can sustain his inner life so that his mind is continually fed throughout the week, and also to prepare himself to enter most fully into the silent worship of a Quaker meeting. We must now look at a question which can puzzle both newcomers and established Friends alike. When is it right to break the silence by some vocal contribution, and what kind of thing can be said that will most help the meeting?

V

TO SPEAK OR NOT TO SPEAK

When I first started attending meeting many years ago one elderly Quaker made clear to me what an awesome thing it was for anyone to take upon himself the responsibility of 'breaking the silence' by actually speaking in meeting. To this Friend, and on this point I entirely agree with her, the uniqueness of a Quaker meeting lies in the fact that it consists of a group of people who willingly engage in a quiet, corporate stillness, something of the venture of which I have attempted to describe in this book. A completely silent meeting is tremendously satisfying, provided always that the silence is alive and creative. 'In the united stillness of a truly "gathered" meeting there is a power known only by experience, and mysterious even when most familiar.'[68]

On the other hand there can be meetings in which the silence is not creative and living, but merely lacking in words. Such gatherings are tersely summed up by L. V. Hodgkin. 'Dead silence leads nowhere. It is not a way, but a wall, a barrier, a padlocked door.'[69] Thomas Green wrote of these two types: 'there is a living silence and dead silence. Acoustically they may be the same, but to the spiritually sensitive there is a profound difference.'[70]

I do not think that one needs to be highly sensitive to detect the difference between living and dead silence; nor am I altogether happy with the view of that old Quaker friend of mine, who laid such stress on the awesome nature of the responsibility of 'breaking the silence' by speech of some kind. My slight dissent from both these well founded views arises from the fact that the way of silent worship is, basically, a most natural one. Having made these mild qualifications, I must stress that I do recognize that there is a real responsibility resting upon a person who speaks in meeting to be truly sensitive to its growing life.

New voices welcomed

The most valuable things said in meeting are those that honestly reflect real experience and are expressed simply: this is true regardless of the age of the person who speaks. As much of this section is a consideration of the difficulties caused by unhelpful ministry I want at the start to stress how greatly meetings can be enriched by the enthusiasm of newcomers: this includes young people who have been brought up in the Society as well as those who have had no previous association with Friends. They all bring with them fresh ways of looking at life.

Like Friends themselves they will wish to respond to the spirit of the meeting, but we should not want them to be so inhibited by the sense of the responsibility of speaking that they feel quite unable to say a word. If, at first glance, we may look rather stuffy respectable people, resistant to new ideas, let me assure readers that this is a misleading impression: I have always been struck by the openness of Friends.

In the Society today there is tremendous respect and admiration for the idealism of young people. The restless questioning that arises from genuine perplexity will be accepted by older Friends as a challenge and a welcome injection of new life into the meeting provided that the speaker is not trying to shock for the sake of shocking. I find among newcomers and young people a real enjoyment and appreciation of the silence. When they speak they generally do so briefly and to the point. In fact they want more silence not less, and are confused when Friends speak too frequently and at great length.

Seventeenth-century experience

A glance at Quaker history will help to set things in perspective. 'For absolutely silent meetings (wherein there is a resolution not to speak) we know not,' says the saintly Isaac Penington, of seventeenth-century Quakerism. He continues, 'but we wait on the Lord, either to feel him in words, or in silence of spirit without words, as he pleaseth'.[71] It is quite clear that the early Friends interpreted their meetings for worship as times when those present waited upon God in the most profound stillness of mind, in a silence sometimes lasting for several hours. They did so always in a spirit of openness, expressed by Robert Barclay as, 'a holy dependence of the mind upon God . . . until words can be brought forth, which are from God's spirit'.[72]

We are also indebted to Robert Barclay for his indication of the variety of people who actually spoke in meeting for ' . . . it is left to the free gift of God to choose any whom he sees meet thereunto, whether rich or poor, servant or master, young or old, yea male and female'.[73] Many of these 'labouring and mechanic men, altogether without learning', affected him so that 'my heart has been often greatly broken and tendered by that virtuous life that proceeded from the powerful ministry of those illiterate men'.[74]

According to another early Friend, Thomas Story, their words could be wide-ranging and include 'doctrine, exposition of the Holy Scriptures, reproof, instruction in morals or whatever tends to the convincement of unbelievers, confirmation of the unstable, edification of the church and body of Christ and perfecting the sanctified in him'.[75] Let me hasten to add that I do not think Thomas Story intended to convey the idea that all

101

these things must be made explicit in every meeting; he was merely noting what sort of things could be expressed in words spoken in meeting.

To a seventeenth-century Friend 'breaking the silence', although he would not have used the phrase, would have meant speaking only when powerfully prompted to do so by the spirit of God.

The Quietist period

Between that first enthusiastic era of Quakerism and our own, lies not only the great gulf between the early Friends' general understanding of the way things are and our way of looking at life (see p. 53), but also the so-called 'quietist period' of Quaker history. The seeds of this were already present in early Quakerism for we find Isaac Penington writing, 'For man is to come into the poverty of Self, into the abasedness, into the nothingness, into the silence of his Spirit before the Lord, into the putting off of all his Knowledge, Wisdom, Understanding, Abilities, all that he is, hath done, or can do . . . '.[76]

During the eighteenth century this tendency had developed to an extreme point where Friends who ministered in meetings, according to John W. Graham, 'laboured to have no thoughts, no purposes of their own . . . in their desperate efforts to reach the Presence, these preachers threw away also what was good in their personalities. They abased themselves, their minds and wills before the Lord. The invitation for ministry must come as God's precious gift without any effort on their part. They sank down into quietness before the Lord, becoming if they could, "Nothing, Nothing" '.[77] Nevertheless, I would not entirely denigrate the 'quietist' period for that would be an unfair judgement; much that is good in modern Quakerism arose at that time. It was, however, during this period that vocal contributions came to be thought of as the terrible responsibility of 'breaking the silence'.

The balance restored

Things slowly changed, first under the impact of the evangelical revival, and second, and with far more important consequences, with the re-emergence towards the close of the nineteenth century of an attitude more closely allied with the origins of Quakerism. So the Society recovered the balance between words and silence in its worship. Our present concern is to look at the position as it is today and ask 'How do vocal contributions arise in our meetings?'

An American Friend, Thomas R. Kelly, who wrote *A Testament of Devotion*, one of the classics of such literature of our age, said in another place, ' . . . words should not break the silence, but continue it. For the Divine Life who was ministering through the medium of silence is the same Life as is now ministering through words. And when such words are truly spoken "in the Life", then when such words cease the *uninterrupted* silence and worship continue, for silence and words have been of one texture, one piece'.[78]

As the rest of this section is going to deal with issues connected with vocal contributions it seems right at this point to pay tribute to those faithful Friends who come regularly to meeting, but never speak. Yet they make a tremendous contribution to the silent worship by their deeply gathered stillness. Their gentle, patient, receptivity of the vocal ministry of other Friends, whether or not it helps them, is a model to us all, and a pointer to the manner in which negative contributions can, by such positive receptivity, be transmuted into a blessing for the whole meeting.

As I have remarked earlier, anyone may speak in a Quaker meeting, provided that this is in response to its developing life.

There is no separated ministry in the Society, although from the earliest time Friends who were observed to have an obvious facility for speaking in 'the ministry', were recognized as 'Publick Friends' and later as 'Recorded Ministers'. In the hope that a wider number of Friends might feel a greater responsibility for speaking in the meeting, the practice was discontinued by London Yearly Meeting in 1924. This act underlines the recognition by modern Friends of the importance of spoken contributions, while they continue to value and appreciate the silence from which speech arises as greatly as any early Friend.

Responding to the life of the meeting

In this section, and several times elsewhere in this book, I have qualified my statement that anyone is welcome to speak in meeting by using some such words as, 'provided it is done in sensitivity to the growing life and spirit of the meeting'. In contrast, readers will have noticed that in the quotations from seventeenth-century sources it was clearly claimed that those who spoke did so as the result of 'waiting upon the Lord', or 'in holy dependence of the mind upon God'. The first Quakers were equally clear that the words they uttered 'are from God's spirit'. My use of a different terminology is quite deliberate, for although I recognize that there are modern Friends who would feel no hesitation in using language largely similar to that of seventeenth-century Friends, I know there are others for whom this would raise grave difficulties. Nevertheless, even they would certainly recognize that speaking in meeting for worship is coloured by a special quality and approach.

I would hope that all Friends would be able to find unity in the general description of the nature of religious experience I have been expressing throughout this book. Namely, that it is a way of looking at our total experience and interpreting it in terms of the transcendence of that experience, so that it calls for a sense of worship and of religious commitment. 'For the intrinsic nature of man's religion is worship' says Peter Berger and he adds, 'It is in worship that the prototypical gesture of religion is realized again and again. This is the gesture in which man reaches out in hope towards transcendence'.[79] I would also hope that Friends would be able to accept Harry Williams' interpretation of the Holy Spirit as, 'The Spirit is ourselves in the depths of what we are . . . this place where God and me mingle indistinguishably'.[80] It is by responding to this sense of transcendence in our deepest being that spoken contributions arise in meeting.

Ministry early in meeting

At the start of any meeting for worship all those present will be joining with one another in the corporate venture of the interior journey. It may be that one of the group will be so deeply sensitive to the unseen, silent, intangible process, and will himself have travelled so swiftly and so far towards the deep still centre, that he will be able, by a few brief words, to assist or promote a movement towards a similar depth in others. But for myself I would feel that only an overwhelming sense of certainty that this is what is required of him, coupled with the greatest caution and real humility, would justify a spoken contribution in the early period of a meeting before it clearly has become deeply gathered. This view I find supported by Thomas Green, who says, 'ministry should ideally, I believe, be an aid to meditation, which at any rate for me, is normally a later stage in a meeting for worship'.[81]

The one possible exception is the offering of vocal prayer, which is sometimes held to be of great value in the opening period of meeting. While I would not deny that such prayer can be beneficial, I would still feel that even this vocal contribution

105

should only be given with the greatest sensitivity and caution.

The preceding paragraphs illustrate the problem of writing about the content and timing of spoken contributions in a meeting for worship. It is so easy to fall into the trap of appearing to suggest that there is a proper sequence which every meeting should follow. Because of the essential spontaneity of Quaker worship there can be no such sequence. I can, for example, envisage circumstances in which some vocal contribution in the early part of a meeting might be appropriate. The same spontaneity also makes it difficult to avoid sounding authoritarian when attempting to indicate the kind of ideas and words that are suitable.

The use of language

I find the following comments from Kathleen Bliss, although written in a quite different context, a most useful general guide. Her words reach me with a freshness and power because they do not come from a Quaker. She writes, 'If language is a creative faculty, then we have to use it boldly to describe for ourselves and others whatever has the ring of truth and genuineness for us. By disciplining this use, bringing to bear on it a necessary economy and sincerity, we examine our lives, finding what frustrates and what enhances our knowledge and practice of truth and love. If we are open to the possibilities of language we will be sensitive to the use of it by others and recognize that others may be speaking of profoundly religious matters without using traditional language.'[82]

Spoken contributions in a Quaker meeting need not be expressed in what is often thought of as devout or religious language, for we are the children of our age, and must necessarily think and speak in the experience, forms of thought, and words of our time. However, our contributions do need to reflect the experience and ideas that are really true for us, because we have lived through them, pondered upon them, considered them most deeply and thus appropriated them for ourselves.

What we say should always have the innate capacity to transcend ordinary human experience although remaining part of it, but nevertheless pointing to an enlarged dimension and vision of life. Trivial language is almost always jarring, though laughter is by no means unknown.

Self-questioning

Anyone who feels drawn to speak should accept the discipline of asking some questions of himself before he opens his mouth. The chief object of these questions is that he shall be clear why he wants to speak. The kind of questions I have in mind are: 'Is the experience or idea I am about to share with my fellow worshippers such that it will contribute to the sensitivity of the life of the meeting and help it to reach an awareness of transcendence? Will my contribution help forward the sense of awe, wonder, adoration, praise and thanksgiving—an affirmation of the splendour and goodness of life and its ultimate purpose in love and truth?'

Such positive contributions will always have the ability to reach and speak to the condition of some, if not all the people in the meeting. As he delivers his message the speaker may know something akin to the experience, so well described by Thomas Kelly 'When one rises to speak in such a (gathered) meeting one has a sense of *being used*, of being played upon, of being spoken through'.[83]

We may be prompted to give a negative answer to the questions I have suggested if we recall the words of Thomas Green, when he said he found it, 'a test of Christian forbearance to be obliged to listen to a homily on some aspect of morality a few minutes after settling down to worship'.[84] If what we are going

to say at any time in meeting is likely to test the Christian forbearance of any of those present, it well may be that our contribution is not really what is needed! Anything that smacks of
self-advertisement, or axe-grinding, or is in the nature of useful
information that we should like to let people know that we
possess, should give rise in us to strong hesitations as to its
suitability, to put it mildly. It is a well established custom that
any individual speaker only makes one contribution to a particular meeting. It is almost impossible to conceive a situation
when departure from this time-honoured tradition would be
justified.

As I have noted earlier, the gifts of experience and insight we
bring to a meeting vary enormously and can be the source of
tremendous enrichment. They will, of course, include many
levels of intellectual and educational achievements, and
differences in the facility with which some of those present are
able to verbalize their thoughts and ideas. The Society needs
constantly to be aware of an anti-intellectual bias, by recog-
nizing the value of thoughtful contributions which can clarify
a religious problem with precision. An example of what I have
in mind is the ministry of a Friend whose deep assimilation of
the Bible illuminates everything that arises in meeting, whose
phraseology is never pious or in any sense conventional; it is
that of a well-informed scholar who feels deeply. It is also,
sadly, true that Friends who have intellectual gifts can be a
burden by speaking too readily, too frequently and too
lengthily, and unwittingly indulging in the habit of 'thinking
aloud' in meeting. Where the Friend concerned clearly has
something constructive to say, this may not be so harmful as
it is in the case of Friends who feel, with less justification, that
the bent of their minds lies in an intellectual direction. Then the
unfortunate habit of 'thinking aloud' degenerates to that of
'rambling aloud', and almost always at great length. I am sure

that such Friends are generally unaware of what they are doing. But any Friend who thinks back on the last few meetings he has attended and asks himself how frequently, and at what length, he has spoken may well be helped to discipline himself. L. V. Hodgkin has written wisely. In a wordy meeting 'each Friend who feels called upon to rise and deliver a lengthy discourse might question himself—or herself—most searchingly, as to whether the message could not be more lastingly given in the fewest possible words or even through his or her personality alone in entire and trustful silence'.[85]

Too much speaking

Some of my readers may feel that I am labouring this point of over-speaking and unhelpful ministry too heavily. The most casual acquaintance with Quaker history, coupled with any wide experience of many modern meetings, sadly produces overwhelming evidence that more meetings are harmed by too much speaking than by too little. If only we all heeded the following advice given by George Fox in his *Epistle* 150 written in 1657. 'None go beyond the measure of the Spirit of God, nor quench it; for when it is quenched, it cannot try things. So if any hath anything upon them to speak, in the life of God stand up, and speak it, if it be but Two or Three words, and sit down.'[86] But even Fox's contempories were insensitive to his advice for Thomas Story writes in his journal of a meeting he attended. 'It was a crowding time . . . there not being for the most part one minute's time between the end of one testimony and the beginning of another, an indecency I have ever disliked'.[87] In terms similar to George Fox, Samuel Bownas wrote 100 years later, 'As thou beginnest with the Spirit, keep to it in thy going on and conclude in it, and this will preserve thee from tiring thy brethren, and causing them to wish for thy silence.'[88]

109

In the Epistle from George Fox from which I have just quoted, he advised Friends 'not to quench the Spirit for where quenched it cannot try things'. Undoubtedly Fox had in mind the kind of ministry that has about it the flavour of the Old Testament prophets who felt compelled, as did the first Friends themselves, 'to declare the Day of the Lord'. All Quaker experience confirms that there will be times in meetings for worship, when sensitivity to the life of the meeting will cause a Friend to feel, with absolute certainty and within the competence of his own experience that what he must say will be likely to disturb the tranquil atmosphere of the meeting if he is to be honest. For utterances in meeting must, if they are to be sincere, express not only what is cheerful, comforting, beautiful and good in our experience, but also what is true, and while that can often be cheerful, it may equally well be uncomfortable as it shakes complacency and challenges us. As I look back over the years, I have recognized the power, helpfulness and value of such ministry, which has carried the meeting to a deeper sense of transcendent values.

The trap of role playing

With hindsight too, I have in all frankness to recognize that I have sometimes felt this kind of demand upon myself and I hope I have responded to it with humility. I also trust that a fear of unpopularity will never keep Friends from so speaking. But with the same frankness I have to admit that I have been conscious of times when I have been a victim of the prophetic syndrome by falling into the trap of role-playing the 'Quaker Minister' and have spoken, while not untruthfully, more from the pleasure of hearing my own voice and registering the dramatic effects my words are having upon the meeting. For a moment it is a satisfying sensation of power, but it swiftly changes to a distasteful sense of play-acting and insincerity.

This is a delicate subject to discuss because Friends rightly encourage all to feel a real responsibility for the spoken ministry. I gladly recognize that, with great faithfulness, and often at considerable cost to themselves, a large number of Friends have responded to this encouragement with sensitivity, to the benefit of their meeting. We should, however, remember that the line between this creative response and a destructive one is, indeed a thin one, for there is in all of us a strong tendency to make judgemental statements about the ideas, attitudes and behaviour of others, by which we endeavour, only too successfully, to boost our egos.

In an earlier section of this book I said that the most deplorable state into which a meeting could degenerate was that of a debating society. Nothing is more likely to bring this state of affairs about than the intrusion of ministry of a party political nature or on a highly controversial subject. People likely to be at a meeting are usually those who hold strong convictions on these subjects, and it is almost impossible for such ministry not to engender a spirit of argument and debate in their minds. They may be sufficiently disciplined so that they do not actually contradict what has been said, but all the same, the spirit of controversy stirred in them will inevitably seep into the sensitive atmosphere of the meeting.

How can we help to save ourselves and protect our meetings? Here I can only speak personally. When I feel prophetic zeal stealing upon me, or sense the temptation to play the role of the 'Quaker Minister', then I feel that I must search my conscience, and question my motives more closely than ever. One clear 'stop' signal for me (not always obeyed I fear) would be the slightest sense that I was tempted to put someone right. To speak or not to speak in these circumstances is made more difficult to decide because there are occasions when a view is expressed which is clearly, although often unwittingly, in-

111

correct; honesty and truthfulness call for some redress. But such ministry requires the most demanding self-examination, the greatest tenderness of spirit and the most careful choice of words, so that the effect will be to take up what is constructive and develop that. Again words from George Fox can help us. 'Who are to be silent and who are to speak,' he writes. 'Now mind where the Watching is, and the Praying is, they are in the Light, in that which silences the Flesh, for words in that leads from the watch. Therefore come to know the watch set before everyone of your mouths.'[89]

The teaching ministry

This self-critical watching also seems to me to apply in several other directions. From time to time one hears older Friends in particular longing for a return to the halcyon days of the teaching ministry. I must confess I am never sure exactly what is meant by this, but I take it that the phrase is intended to cover spoken contributions that convey instruction on the nature of the Quaker interpretation of the Christian faith, especially in its doctrinal aspects. On the surface this may seem to be a wholly admirable objective, but in practice it can so easily slip into something not far short of sermons and mini-lectures, the very things that Barclay warned seventeenth-century Friends against in his picturesque phrase 'conned and gathered stuff'. I write with some feeling, because for several years I attended a meeting where, with great regularity, the same Friend, at the same time each Sunday literally gave the meeting a lesson. This was not helped by the hectoring way he had of speaking, coupled with the hint that we had obviously not listened properly the previous week, so that he felt obliged to repeat himself. Some of what he said was excellent, for he had a good and scholarly mind, but the spirit and intention

112

with which he gave it, destroyed for many of us the constructive parts of his ministry.

Everything turns on the attitude and intention in which ministry with a teaching content is given. If it is in response to the spirit in the meeting, and is offered in such a way that it deepens the sense of awe, wonder and awareness of transcendence; then it can be creative and valuable, and will speak to the condition of those present so that their 'minds will be fed'. If, on the contrary, its underlying attitude is to use the meeting as a kind of classroom and to take advantage of a captive audience to give instruction in Quakerism, Christianity or any other religion or philosophy, then, almost without exception, the speaking is out of place, and more likely to hinder the growth of contemplation and worship: the silent accompaniments of the journey to the deep still centre.

Closely associated with the problems of the teaching ministry is the reading aloud of the Bible, or other similar books in meeting. Nothing can be more creative to a spirit of deep worship than a brief reading of some verses from the Bible, when they have been chosen in response to the growing, corporate spirit of the meeting. But, so often, a Bible reading, plus usually a not particularly helpful commentary upon it, seems to be injected into, rather than arising from the meeting. This unnatural use of the scriptures arises partly from the fact that not all Friends are so familiar with them as was at one time the case. One gets the impression that the passage has probably been looked up before the meeting, because the Friend in question could not repeat it from memory (the old Quaker ideal for the use of scriptures in meeting), or would not easily be able to find the passage he wanted. So again I would ask myself, or any other Friend, to be specially self-critical when he feels drawn to read from the scriptures. One of the worst uses of the Bible in meeting was demonstrated some years ago in the meeting I was then attending. If it seemed to be 'in danger' of being completely silent, one of the Elders could be counted on to read a passage from *Isaiah*, just to make sure that something was said, particularly if newcomers were present. Little did she realize that one of the delights of the enquirer who approaches Quakerism is to discover the simplicity and beauty of a silent way of worship.

The Advices and queries

Sooner or later a newcomer to a Quaker meeting will be present when someone reads from the *Advices and queries*. They are among the choicest pieces of Quaker literature, and are revised in each generation by the whole Society, so they most nearly reflect the corporate insights of Quakers.

> The *Advices and queries* are intended for use in our meetings and for private devotion. Their use will vary in different meetings according to the needs of members. Generally it will be helpful to arrange for the reading of the *Advices and queries* in meetings for worship over a specific period, while taking care that such reading should not be carried out within too limited a time.[90]

The instruction from *Church Government* provides for flexibility in the use of *Advices and queries* in Quaker worship. In practice I feel there is a thin line that divides their constructive use from their negative use. There is a tendency to read too much at one time. It is my experience that in meeting one is only able to absorb a very brief amount of anything that is read. Further the *Advices and queries* tend to be read early in the meeting, at a time when, as I have already indicated, spoken ministry of any kind is not generally most helpful, although I would remind my readers that I have also indicated that if offered with great sensitivity it may be of benefit. Some Friends, I know, do find a reading from the *Advices and queries*

114

early in the meeting very constructive as it assists the direction of their worship. On the whole, I must say that this has not been my experience. Again I can make my point best by illustrating it from something that happened to me on arrival at meeting one Sunday, breathless but triumphant at not actually being late! The Friend acting as doorkeeper thrust a copy of the *Advices and queries* into my hand, telling me that I was to read a particular passage. I surreptitiously looked at the passage as I sat in meeting: as the silence deepened, I became more and more convinced that, though required in order to keep up to date with our readings, the particular passage was not in tune with the growing life of the meeting that day. I sat still and waited: one or two Friends contributed most helpfully. The tenor of their remarks made me more certain than ever that the passages I had been asked to read were not appropriate; at the same time I became equally sure that a quite different passage would speak to the condition of the meeting in a way that probably nothing else could. So I read that passage, and from remarks made to me by Friends afterwards, it would seem that I had been rightly sensitive to the life of the meeting on that occasion.

Poetry and hymns

While on the subject of things read in meeting I feel I must say something about the use of poetry. Here again a poem that a Friend has made truly his own, and is able to recite simply and sincerely, without histrionics and in response to the growth of the meeting, can be most moving and of enormous benefit. I have been blessed for some years by the ministry of a Friend, who because of her knowledge and understanding of Shakespeare, is able to use his beautiful language and ideas to make briefly, but tellingly, the depth of his insight available to us all.

Sometimes, however, one's experience of poetry read or said

in meeting is far from helpful: this is usually when a Friend brings with him his favourite collection, and reads one of the most abstruse poems in it. Though it may mean something to him through his close acquaintance with it, it is not likely to be assimilated by the meeting on first hearing. This either has the effect of starting the meeting off on an intellectual chase after the meaning, or of irritating those of us who can hardly understand one line, or worst of all, in inducing the reader to expound at great length, what he thinks the poem means. Perhaps it is hardly fair while dealing with poetry to mention at this point the old Friend who, from time to time, produced from his pocket a particularly unfortunate hymn book (at one time much favoured by Friends) and read a hymn. Because he was a Friend from birth and was, therefore, steeped in the Quaker tradition of not preparing material beforehand for use in meeting, he always prefaced his reading with the remark: 'By a strange coincidence I have brought a hymn book with me this morning and feel guided to read hymn so and so.' At this point he opened the book and out fluttered a book-marker from the chosen place. Now the strange thing was, that although he was by no means a good public speaker, his sincere but faltering comments upon the often appalling words of the hymn really did convey a sense of transcendence, because they were a true expression of his real and deeply held convictions, which would have been far more effective without the hymn!

Reference to hymns naturally raises the question of singing in meeting. Although from time to time hymns have been sung in meetings by all Friends present, the general experience is that they are not helpful, largely because their use required a certain degree of planning and because the words themselves may be difficult for all Friends to sing with sincerity. Now and again an individual Friend has sung a hymn, unaccompanied, as his vocal contribution. Recently I was present at the daily meeting for worship in Pendle Hill. The meeting was deeply gathered when a woman Friend sang in English a Bach chorale. It was the most perfect expression of the life of the meeting. But then, she could sing, and this is not always true of Friends who offer such contributions. Also in America on a previous visit I remember a girl coming into meeting with a guitar. Later she played and sang but on this occasion I had the feeling that, although she sang well, yet her contribution was injected into the meeting rather than being prompted from its deep life.

The call to speak

Having looked at the various kinds of vocal contributions to a meeting and the ways in which they arise, we are now in a position to consider what further indications there are which can help us to know when one should speak. It has long been widely held, and still is, that a quickening of the heart beat that accompanies the growing clarification in one's mind of something that could be said, is a sure sign that it should be said. Whilst I should feel a strong reluctance to accept this particular physical effect as an infallible guide, I would at the same time be reluctant to disregard it entirely. Clearly some people do feel that it constitutes a useful, if uncomfortable indication to them of their responsibility. I have yet to meet the Friend who has never at some time or other been aware of this condition. The first Quakers did not see in this a call to speak but rather the response to the awesome presence of God.

Today with our knowledge of the effects of the release of adrenalin into the blood stream, as part of nature's way of preparing us to face dangers, known and unknown, we are less inclined to accept this physical condition as a positive call to speak. All I can say is that sometimes when my heart has thumped its hardest, I have had to recognize that the ministry

I gave was most certainly not in the life, whereas on other occasions it has been. Similar heart beatings have been my experience in situations far different from any Quaker gathering. It is also true that I have found myself speaking in meeting, sometimes constructively and sometimes not, when I have been perfectly calm physically.

I think one is more soundly helped to know whether or not to speak by allowing the piece of possible ministry to develop gently in one's mind, and at the same time testing it by the kind of questioning I have suggested earlier. Many Friends at this point will turn for guidance to their experience of the spirit in the depths of their being, 'this place where God and me mingle indistinguishably'. Whatever terminology we use we shall want to hold our embryonic message in the quiet still centre, for as John W. Graham has said, ' . . . ministry can only rise out of silence, and expresses what has happened in the silence. It cannot arise beyond our experience, but it may rise as high'.[91] For whatever anyone says in meeting they will use their own words, experiences and ideas, but they will be speaking not for themselves only, but on behalf of the gathered company.

A Friend to whom I sent the first draft of this book comments upon his experience of speaking in meeting as follows: 'As I get nearer to the point of rising to speak, not only does my heartbeat rise (as you say, not a trustworthy sign of the Holy Spirit at work) but I have a mounting sense of mental activity—real excitement: thoughts colliding, falling into a moving pattern, joining to make new sense. The Inner Light becomes almost a physical reality; it flickers over the content of the mind—and by mind I mean the whole content of both feeling and thoughts—and then comes to rest in a way that lights up the whole: so that on some rare occasions the statement I am about to make is presented to me whole, and I don't have to make my way through phraseology; it is "given".'

While I would hesitate to describe my own experience in such vivid terms, I do recognize in what he writes something of what happens before I speak, and I think that this may be true of the experience of others.

Delayed ministry

Many years ago I recall a conversation with a wise Friend and colleague, and together we invented the phrase 'delayed action ministry', The idea is presented in more stately terms in *Christian Faith and Practice*. What we had in mind was that some thought may come to one at any time during the week, and immediately one recognizes that here is the germ of valuable ministry. The more one reflects upon this probably commonplace thought, and sees how it is open to a religious interpretation in terms of transcendence, the more the chances are that one arrives at meeting with a beautifully prepared piece of ministry. Then there is an overwhelming temptation to deliver it while it is fresh in one's mind. The condition of the meeting may indicate that this is what is required. But it well may not. In that case one needs great sensitivity and self-discipline not to speak. However, after some weeks, or even months, the time may well come when one knows intuitively that this long stored ministry is exactly what the meeting needs.

Some Friends who speak rather too frequently in meeting do so because they feel that others are unwilling to share the responsibility. Without detracting one word from what I said earlier about the faithful Friends who never speak yet make such a positive contribution by their silent reverent presence, one can distinguish another type of silent Friend, who has the ability to speak but rarely or never does so. Perhaps he should ask himself whether he should consider that in response to the life of the meeting he could sometimes contribute vocally.

One of the times when one is most conscious of the sense of

'breaking the silence', is when one is the first to speak in meeting. Guidance on this point seems to me exactly similar to that I have indicated when considering the question of the possibility of ministry early in a meeting, plus, of course, the usual questioning that relates to all spoken contributions. In later ministry one always can gain at least a pointer to the possible suitability of one's contribution by one extra and obvious question, namely, whether what one feels prompted to say is an extension and fulfilment of previous ministry. Alternatively, is it starting a new line of thought? As a general principle I think one can say that it is usually helpful if later ministry can build on, and develop what has come earlier; but no hard and fast rule can be made about this. It could be that earlier contributions had been somewhat discursive and unhelpful. Then it would be useful to try and lead the ministry into a new direction more in keeping with the meeting's deeper creative life. This might be achieved by overlooking what had already been said, or by seeing whether there was a way of re-interpreting it in a positive way. This, of course, needs to be done with great sensitivity. There is a tendency in some meetings in America, and not unknown in this country, for Friends to 'respond to messages'. I find this practice difficult to accept, partly because the response follows rather quickly, and partly because it so often consists of a re-interpretation of the message in terms in which the interpreter wished the earlier speaker had spoken.

One thing of which I am firmly convinced is that, if the spoken contributions tend to drift aimlessly over a variety of unconnected topics, then the meeting has not been truly gathered even if each may have been good in itself. For meetings tend to get the kind of ministry they deserve in the light of the quality of the gathered silence that they achieve and respond to. Even in such a meeting it is possible that someone who has really found the true centre, despite all distractions, can often be so sensitive to the state of the meeting that he is able with a few words, sincerely felt and spoken, to bring the most ungathered meeting to a genuine sense of togetherness in its closing period. But the ability to do this does rest on the conditions I have just mentioned; a contrived effort to draw a meeting into unity can be immediately recognized as such.

Vocal prayer in meeting

In times past and not infrequently now, vocal prayer could be the most effective means of helping a meeting towards deep unity. I have already touched on the difficulties that many Friends experience with vocal prayer in meeting, for this involves a person having to pray, not only on his own behalf, but in the sense of the corporate body of Friends. In the previous section I made reference to new ways of thinking of prayer which may help to ease the hesitation of some Friends. There are still very many Friends for whom prayer to God is a simple reality, and when they contribute vocal prayer in meeting, which is sincerely offered, it can be gratefully accepted by the whole meeting, even if some present would find this contribution unnatural for them. For prayer understood as concerned and compassionate thinking in the light of the transcendence of human values is a ground for unity. This can be increased when prayer is also conceived as a sense of natural, joyful communion in inner silence. As a concrete example of what I have in mind I can point to a meeting's common desire to give its spiritual support to one of its members who is sick or facing bereavement. Each member of the meeting will pray for the person concerned in his own way, which will differ greatly from member to member. But all will gather and hold the sick or bereaved Friend, first in the stillness of themselves, and then in the stillness at the centre of the deep life of the meeting. So the diversity of their various conceptions of prayer will ultimately enrich and not divide.

The same is true of other words spoken in a meeting for worship, for as Pierre Lacout has finely said, 'If nevertheless I speak, it is to communicate with souls whose silence is in unison with mine and who hear the Silence of God in the words I use. If I speak again it is to awaken to this silence souls ready to receive it. But I am convinced that neither the written nor the spoken word will ever be as precious as Silence. For, in the soul dwelling in Silence, God himself is Silence.'[92]

The rediscovery of silence

This has been a long section because I feel that what the Society needs more than anything else is to rediscover the uniqueness of its silent way of worship. This recovery means the honest facing of the problems of too much talking in meeting. In this section I have only touched briefly upon the type of ministry that is creative and useful because comments upon it have been implicit in what I have written in the other sections. Some Friends, especially those in our numerous small meetings, may well be feeling that, far from attempts to discourage ministry, they would like more advice on how to promote it. I fully appreciate the problems of the small meeting, where members are so well known to each other that they can have a fairly shrewd guess at the kind of spoken contribution any one of them is likely to make. It is my conviction that, where such small groups are prepared to dedicate themselves to the effective use of a creative, living silent exploration of the interior life, this might be the greatest hope for the full recovery of the amazing fact of Quaker worship. There are some ways in which the larger community of Friends can help and these I will mention in the next section.

VI

THE QUAKER COMMUNITY

Like all human groups, the Society of Friends has developed an 'in' language of its own, that can be confusing to the newcomer, and also unintentionally make him feel a bit of an intruder. Wherever possible I have tried to avoid this Quaker jargon, or to explain it when it has been necessary. Even so I expect a number of these special words have slipped into my writing because I am so accustomed to them, that I haven't noticed them. So I have used the word meeting only to refer to the meeting for worship, but in fact it, and words associated with it, are used in several different ways by Friends. One of the most widespread uses is to apply it in a loose kind of way to the group of people who are associated with a Quaker meeting for worship in a locality. It can also be used in a more precise manner to mean the people who have actually joined the Society as members and are associated with a particular meeting. It can further mean the members of a particular meeting gathered to conduct its business and make decisions. So it is possible to hear at the close of a meeting for worship an announcement to the effect that, 'The meeting has decided to hold a public meeting to let people in the district know about Quaker faith and practice'. There are other uses of the word which need not concern us now.

What I want to consider in this section is the meeting as a community of people which has the centre of its life in the Quaker meeting for worship, but which also exists as a community, within the wider community of society in general. It is impossible to think of a group of Friends, and others meeting together for worship but having no further links with each other. While in the strict sense of the word community can only be applied to the meeting as a community in a general way, yet in practice its outline is quite clear. The extent to which the meeting is able to become a real community of people who love and care for one another, and at the same time is not closed in on itself but open to people beyond it, vitally affects the quality of the meeting for worship, as conversely that particular activity also vitally affects the quality of the meeting as a community.

When Quakers finally settled as their official title the Religious Society of Friends one deliberate reason for the choice was that they felt themselves to be friends gathered in a society which had its basis in a religious outlook on life, and one of its practical emphases in ordinary human friendship. But they never were, and are not now content to be just ordinary friends, for the Society urges its members 'to know one another in the things that are eternal'. By this it means that they should recognize in one another a willingness to be open to each other in encounter at the deepest levels of life in the way that I have described earlier. It does not mean that each Friend has to be involved with every other Friend in a deep personal relationship; apart from anything else, this would be impossible because of demands on people's time and energy. Nor does it mean that every Friend is necessarily expected to like every other Friend equally, for tastes and interests vary considerably. But it does mean that each Friend is committed to a sense of loving care and concern for the deepest well-being of his fellow Friends, and also to share with them the conviction that this kind of relationship, while firmly part of human life, always transcends it and points to life's real meaning and purpose.

124

Interdependence of worship and life

It can easily be seen how a community based on this ideal makes such an important contribution to the Quaker meeting for worship. The first practical way in which it does this is that its members go to meeting with some regularity so that they form the core of the meeting for worship, which provides an essential and valuable common ground as its point of departure and growing life. But Quakers attend their meetings not primarily from a sense of duty, but rather because they want to. For there, in the special way I have outlined, they are drawn into a profound meeting with one another, which they interpret religiously as communion with life, love, truth and God. So the meeting for worship and the Quaker community are interdependent upon each other—you can't have one without the other. This is not to say that someone cannot derive great benefit from Quaker worship unless he is also involved in the general life of the Quaker community. However, if he is really going to find his spiritual home in the Society of Friends I feel certain that, in addition to going to meeting, he will also want in some degree, which varies from person to person, to be caught up in the life of the local Quaker community.

But in what does this local community consist? Conditions vary greatly from meeting to meeting. They are obviously, affected by their actual situation, such as those in large cities and suburban areas, and those in county towns and rural districts, where members may live scattered over a wide area. From time to time throughout the Society's history, and in the present, some groups of Friends have lived in small communes, but these are exceptional. Most Friends live as families in their own homes, or as single people in various kinds of accommodation. They earn their living in a great variety of ways. While predominantly middle class, they are by no means exclusively so. It is sometimes alleged that the Quaker way of

125

life and worship are specially suited to people inclined to be intellectual. I do not think this is true, for while Quakerism admittedly attracts such people, it also appeals to many others, especially those who enjoy religious freedom and like to think for themselves. Because of the Quaker emphasis that religion needs to be seen as a way of life, it makes a strong appeal to those who want a practical faith. It is not for nothing that Quakerism has been described as 'the do-it-yourself religion'!

Friendship

How then can such a loose-knit body of people be in any way described as a community? It is my conviction that the clue to the Quaker community lies in two words: friendship and communication. One obvious feature of any meeting is the general atmosphere of warmth and friendship that pervades its life. Many members of the meeting establish good and particular personal relationships and enjoy each other's company in ordinary human companionship and everyday pleasures. These friendships tend to overlap with others in a meeting. Clearly people will be specially drawn to each other by shared interests, although groups must be aware of the danger of becoming a clique. But such friendships are not exclusive, and any newcomer who desires it, will speedily be drawn into the group with which, in the first place, he finds the closest identity, and little by little he will come to know more and more people throughout the meeting.

Just as Friends are not content to limit their friendships among themselves to a superficial level, neither will they wish to limit their friendships with interested newcomers. For they are convinced that real personal relationships can, and do, release people from a narrow confined life-style into a full and joyful one, in which they can really be alive. In this respect the newcomer has as much to contribute to Friends as they have to give to him, so it is not surprising that they gladly welcome him. To escape superficiality does not mean falling into solemnity. On the contrary, it leads to authentic living, which is where true happiness, joy and fun are to be found, because people have discovered the confidence of being absolutely themselves through their relatedness to others. For some strange reason Quakers are often thought by the public to be good and kind, even painfully so, but at the same time, as essentially joyless people with no sense of humour. Some Quakers, of course, are a bit like that, but by and large they tend to be cheerful, responsible, well integrated, and essentially loving human beings.

One Quaker tradition that we should carefully maintain is the use of our homes as places of friendship and hospitality. Modern conditions, with many people living alone in small apartments, or only one member of the family being a Friend, do tend to weigh against the earlier habit of open hospitality but any Friend with the facilities for inviting members or newcomers to his home, can make an enormous contribution to the Quaker community. An added modern problem is the fear that, if you go out to pay a social visit on a Friend, you find him deeply engrossed in his pet television programme. The meeting will from time to time arrange social gatherings of various kinds in the meeting house, or in the house of a local Friend. To all such events the newcomer is most warmly welcomed.

Communication

Communication is my second clue word that indicates the character of the Quaker community. Friends are convinced that one of the most important ways of discovering God is in and through their relationship with others. The Society is realistic about this as part of the thirteenth Query indicates

127

10

when it asks, 'Do you respect that of God in each one, though it may be expressed in unfamiliar ways or may be difficult to discern?'[93] One of the ways of seeking that of God in people is by being alert and sensitive to their needs. Unfortunately it is so easy to mistake the signals sent out by others as signs of confidence, whereas in reality they are signals of distress.

The importance of being able to distinguish other people's signals was brought home to me through Stevie Smith's poem, 'Not waving but drowning'. It relates to a man who, while swimming, got out of his depth. People watching thought he was larking about and waving from bravado. When they discovered their mistake they blamed the cold water that had affected his heart.

> Oh no no no it was too cold always
> (Still the dead man lay moaning)
> I was much too far out all my life
> And not waving but drowning[94]

One reason that holds a Quaker meeting together in real friendship is the emphasis the Society places on personal relationships. This common concern gives reality to the concept of the Quaker community, where our ideals can be seen to be both true and practical. It also means that the community, which through its members' wide interests is always overlapping and interpenetrating other non-Quaker groups, is a continuous preparation in ordinary life for the particular activity of worship, where the signals of transcendence are most clearly focussed and interpreted. Quakers take seriously the New Testament call to the early Christian communities: 'Little children love one another,' and the fact that the pagan world in which they lived commented, 'See how these Christians love one another.' Surely if there is any validity in worship it must,

128

at least, reflect itself in the loving quality of life of the community that practises it.

Quaker groups

Though loose and flexible, the Quaker community is not without its simple structures which are freely adopted by members in order to strengthen its life. Several times in this book I have remarked that discussion, debate and argument, and to a certain extent even instruction, are out of place in and disruptive of, the meeting for worship, but that they have their place elsewhere. According to its size, and the needs of its members, a local meeting will arrange a variety of different groups to cater for their requirements. Most meetings from time to time will hold study and discussion groups. These will range widely in the matters they consider, covering anything from the study of the Bible, Quaker faith, life and history, to current issues of social and political concern; local, national and international. In these groups the fresh insights of the newcomer are most welcome, and he too will gain a valuable understanding of the Quaker way of looking at life.

In addition, many meetings will hold small worship-fellowship groups in private homes, and these can be of particular help to the newcomer. Due to their informality he may feel more quickly at ease in them than in a large meeting. The fact that they are opportunities in which he can meet people in a relaxed social atmosphere, also gives him a chance to ask questions about Quaker faith and practice and worship that have been puzzling him.

Incidentally, wherever possible, a newcomer should be encouraged to visit neighbouring meetings, as they will be pleased to welcome him, and he will widen his understanding of Quaker worship by seeing it practised by another group of Friends. I often feel that the newcomer may require particular help after attending his first few meetings for the novelty of this way of worship will by then have worn off. He should not fear to speak of his difficulties, nor should Friends be too reticent in taking the initiative by asking in a sensible, normal way how he is settling into our way of worship. The newcomer will best be helped by frank and honest replies to his questions, rather than by the kind of proper answer that some Friends seem to feel they ought to give.

Some useful experiments are also going on with encounter type groups, usually called worship-sharing groups, where, under competent leadership, a group of people can speak frankly and freely of their experiences in the atmosphere of worship but without discussion. This sort of group is clearly not for everyone, but some do find them useful and speak highly of their value in helping them to cope with personal problems, providing them with a sense of support, and also as a way of becoming integrated into the wider life of the Society, and specially in enabling them to make a better use of meeting for worship.

Throughout the Society, there are Friends who feel a particular dedication to pray for people who are sick: where there are a sufficient number of such Friends in any particular meeting or district, they join together as a prayer group with this special intention in mind.

While I would want the Society to be particularly careful about radically changing the Quaker way of worship, I do see the necessity of experiment with change. Small groups, such as I have just described seem to me the ideal setting for experiment in possible new ways of approaching Quaker worship, which might be held in addition to the ordinary meeting but not as a replacement for it. The use of music and drama and adaptations of other types of Christian and even non-Christian worship, could well be included in such experiments.

Deepening the spiritual life

Every now and again one hears of individual Friends speaking of their desire for the deepening of the spiritual life of the Society. Small groups of the kind I have just described, plus larger area conferences which can devote a whole weekend to thought on a particular issue, are among the practical ways in which this objective can be achieved. The growth of the practice of residential weekends for Friends and others (which provide for the care of children) from a wide area is one major sign of the renascence of Quakerism.

It must be obvious that I am in general sympathy with the concern for a greater depth of spiritual life otherwise I should not have written a book the two-fold object of which is to commend the Quaker way of worship as a valid one for modern people, and also to see if there are ways in which we can make better use of silent worship. Nevertheless, the way in which this desire for a deeper quality of spiritual life is so often expressed leads me to wonder whether the Friends calling for it are not, unconsciously, wanting to find a kind of 'spiritual formula', which, once discovered, will quickly bring the whole Society to greater depth. There is an incipient danger here, for I am inclined to think that such an attitude to life is often an unconscious attempt to escape from the natural, though extremely demanding, path of seeking depth through ordinary everyday living and seeing such experience as that which can be interpreted in terms of transcendence. It must be followed, of course, by the commitment to live our everyday lives in the light of the vision of transcendence.

When I am overcome with a desire for spirituality, which I later recognize as spurious, it is always because I am trying to avoid the demand upon me to set aside my pride, and accept the need to be reconciled with a particular person. In view of this I cannot help but notice that some Friends who press

131

most strongly for a deeper spiritual life, frequently betray in their behaviour towards people an attitude that inhibits them from living in love, sympathy, acceptance and understanding with others. In such circumstances it is my responsibility, and theirs, to respond to the present opportunities for the practice of loving relations afforded by the existence of the Quaker community.

A Friend who takes seriously his part in the Society will, as far as he is able, use all the many opportunities available to him for individual reading and study of Quaker, Christian and other religious literature. Such material he will find in the meeting house library, or the libraries at Friends House and Wood-brooke. In addition, he can make use of his public library and of the enormous number of paperback books on religion and philosophy and related topics, not forgetting the insights he can gain from literature and modern novels. Further, he can broaden his mind through the sensible use of television and radio. In similar ways he can sensitize his emotions through seeing films and plays and listening to music. The important thing for Friends and newcomers alike is to use all these things to broaden their outlook, and not to concentrate only on those aspects that confirm their prejudices. Many a study group has foundered on shared prejudices! But in the end it will be the transcendent quality of his life, achieved partly through these disciplines, that will persuade other Friends of the genuineness of his call for deeper spirituality, and attract them to pursue these things for themselves.

Elders and Overseers

The Society has recognized that some of its members have a particular sensitivity to those qualities in the life of the meeting and in the Friends who belong to it, that are likely to develop its deepest spiritual power. Friends recognized as having this sensitivity are appointed as Elders and they now serve for three-year periods. Upon them is laid a special responsibility to care for the devotional and spiritual life of the members and to do all they can to promote its growth. They have a similar responsibility (although shared by all Friends) for the meeting for worship itself. It is to the Elders that Friends and newcomers alike can look for advice and counsel, not only on religious issues in general, but in particular for guidance and encouragement about such matters as speaking in meeting. The Society is greatly indebted to the loving care and devotion in which many of these Friends have carried out their duties.

An unforseen and unfortunate consequence of the discontinuance of the practice of recording ministers has been a growing tendency to appoint Friends as Elders because of the helpfulness of their ministry. Others when appointed to the office feel that they have a duty to speak regularly. It cannot be said strongly enough that there is no more responsibility resting on an Elder to speak in meeting than that which rests on all Friends. A second unfortunate tendency regarding Elders is to place too great an emphasis on the negative side of their responsibilities. So one hears of being Eldered which, to put it bluntly, means to be taken to task, ever so gently, for speaking unsuitably in meeting. A third unfortunate fact (revealed by a questionnaire on worship sent to members of the Friends Home Service Committee) is that it is all too often true that some of the Elders themselves are the Friends who speak too frequently and at too great a length in meeting.

The idea has also got around, although there is no truth in it, that to be appointed an Elder is the acknowledgement of long and faithful service to the meeting: consequently, not to be reappointed is a terrible blow to the spiritual self-esteem of the Friend concerned. After a period of service many wise Elders have asked to be released for at least a period of time, in order to break the continuity of their service. Elders are not necessarily elderly. Sensitivity, wisdom and insight are the gifts required and these are to be found in Friends of all ages.

Other Friends are appointed as Overseers, who care for the practical life of the Quaker community, and play an extremely important part in it. Both these groups of Friends will feel a particular responsibility for the needs of smaller meetings in their area, to which we must now give some attention.

Small meetings

Much that I have said in this section applies easily to large meetings but not so easily to small ones, whose few members are so busily engaged in keeping even the minimal requirements of Quaker organization going, that they have little time to engage in extra groups. It is here that the wider structure of the Society can help them, especially by seeing that such meetings for worship are regularly visited from time to time, by Friends who are sensitive to their difficulties, and undertake the visit in a spirit of caring. I loved to hear Thomas Green tell of the occasion (not recorded in his Swarthmore Lecture) when he visited a tiny country meeting. On going up the path to the meeting house he noticed two other 'weighty' Friends arriving from neighbouring meetings, also under a concern to visit. As Tom said, 'I knew it was going to be a race as to which of the three of us would speak first.' After the briefest possible time Friend A rose, and delivered a lengthy and obviously prepared address. Despite his physical prowess as a speaker, even he had to pause for breath, and while he was doing so, Friend B leaped to his feet, watch in hand, saying, 'Friend A thee has had thy innings and it's my turn now.' Then addressing the three local Friends present he added, 'If Thomas Green speaks take no notice of him—he's a Unitarian!'

While this story is not without its humour in that it powerfully demonstrates the human frailty of Quakers, it well illustrates how not to visit a small meeting. Having spoken of the difficulties they face, I must record the fact that one of the best meetings I ever attended was a small one, and I am constantly amazed by the vitality to be found in many of them. Their members frequently make much more strenuous efforts to visit one another in their homes, and are often more healthily involved with other non-Quaker groups in their village or town, than members of bigger meetings which are prone to be somewhat self-contained.

One of the most difficult questions to answer relates to the ideal size for a Quaker meeting for worship. Opinions vary tremendously, and this was confirmed in answers to the questionnaire to which I have referred earlier. While there was general agreement that two Friends meeting together could hold an authentic Quaker meeting, it was recognized that regular groups of less than about eight Friends might find worship after the manner of Friends somewhat of a strain; but such views were always qualified by remarks to the effect that it all depended on whether they became truly gathered and really loved and cared for each other. The ideal number seemed to be between 20 and 50, but Friends were obviously reluctant to dogmatize on exact figures.

Any number over 50 was felt to be getting too big, although one Friend said 'the bigger the better'. There was wide consensus in the view that the ideal group should be of such a size for all attending to know one another; one Friend added the qualification that the ideal group would be one in which everybody could be seen and heard.

The value of a meeting house

This seems to be the right point to take up again the issue of whether or not Quakers should spend money on building new meeting houses, or adapting other accommodation for the purposes of a Quaker meeting. Here again opinions differ, some Friends feeling that the right answer is to develop the idea of the 'house church' with meetings held in the homes of Friends. Others are perplexed for, while they feel it un-Quakerly to spend money on building meeting houses, and certainly on elaborate ones, they nevertheless see the value in a meeting having its own premises. This is a view strongly held by members of meetings gathering in a rented room.

From my own experience of extension work I have no doubt whatever, that if we want new people to join the Society, we shall not as a general rule encourage them to do so, by asking them to attend meetings in private houses. This points to the need for some type of public premises. My observations of the prevailing attitude of Friends leads me to think that Friends see the desirability of spending money on the building of new meeting houses, or the adaptation of existing accommodation, as an investment in the spiritual future of the Society. They are aware that in the light of current building costs, either type of building will not be inexpensive. They therefore desire to achieve, as economically as possible, meeting houses that can be used for a variety of social and community purposes, both Quaker and non-Quaker, during the week, as well as for meeting for worship on Sundays. There is a growing desire to have premises that provide accommodation for resident wardens. The idea that Quakers might share accommodation provided on an ecumenical basis attracts some interest but, at the moment, it could hardly be described as a strong concern of Friends as a whole.

Ecumenical involvement

This reference to possible ecumenical involvement prompts me to make several comments about the relation of the Society

136

of Friends to other branches of the Christian church as far as worship is concerned. The first of these is that the Society of Friends has a responsibility to the church in particular and people in general to preserve its particular and unique form of worship based on a living growing silence. There are some Friends who are inclined to feel that Quaker worship could be enriched in a Christian direction by the introduction of the use of bread and wine in a symbolic re-enactment of the Lord's Supper. To my way of thinking this would entirely change the nature of Quaker worship, which in its present simple form is truly sacramental: for it is always an activity that has in mind the sacrificial nature of love, actualized by the way in which Jesus met his death, as a supreme signal of transcendence. One of the important reasons why Friends have not used outward sacraments, and in particular the Lord's Supper or Holy Communion, is that they have always been aware, in their meetings for worship, when they are deeply gathered, of the sense of the living spirit of Jesus with them, and they see no reason for outward signs to convey this presence.

This gentle, unstructured approach allows people to whom highly ritualized sacraments are clearly a hindrance to find a way into worship that is valid for them. In view of the tremendous emphasis on the ecumenical movement current in all branches of the church I feel that a two-fold change is called for in the traditional Quaker approach towards outward sacraments. First, we Quakers must forgo our complacent attitude that they are unnecessary 'props', which, to adapt Fox's alleged advice to William Penn about his sword, the sacramental Christian should 'wear as long as he canst'! In place of this implicit Quaker view we must recognize that the use of outward sacraments by our fellow Christians are valid acts of worship, as real and as effective as any Quaker meeting, and to be treated by us with respect and reverence. At the same time we must hold firmly to our traditional disuse of them in our own meetings. The second change in the Quaker view that I feel is required is that when a Friend, or a newcomer, expresses the wish to participate in some form of Holy Communion, as a supplement to his regular sharing in Quaker worship, he should do so, and not be made to feel guilty as a kind of second-class Quaker.

These two changes in Quaker outlook can, I realize, cause considerable difficulties to some of our fellow Christians, for I am first asking them for the recognition that Quaker worship is a valid sacramental act, fulfilling spiritually what has been interpreted as the wish of Jesus for his followers. Secondly, I am asking that a Quaker, who has not been baptised, should be allowed to take Holy Communion if he so wishes. Many churches are already willing for this to happen but some are not. Until these changes on the part of Quakers and of our fellow Christians are achieved there can, in my view, be no final reality for Friends in the ecumenical movement.

I realize that the changes in attitude for which I am asking also raise considerable difficulties for the Society of Friends which has always held that the gift of God's grace does not depend on outward and visible signs administered by an ordained and separated priesthood; the latter still largely a male preserve. But Quakers are not entirely without outward and visible signs in their worship, such for example as their insistence on the equality of the contribution of men and women, the essential simplicity of their meeting houses, and the use of silence. Changes of attitude among many of our fellow Christians towards the nature of sacraments do, I feel, go a long way to helping Quakers to accept the view I have advanced.

Types of worship

I believe the church as a whole has to provide at least four types of worship which should be open to all those who try to live in the spirit of Jesus, in order to meet the conditions and temperaments of contemporary people. Briefly stated they are: (i) the Catholic tradition of worship which would include the High Anglican; (ii) the Free Church tradition which would include the Middle and Low Church Anglican; (iii) the kind of spirit-filled worship of the pentecostal evangelical groups; and (iv) silent non-liturgical or unprogrammed worship. What would be absolutely disastrous would be a move towards a kind of omelette of Christian worship which tried to provide at one go for all tastes by a mixture of all these traditions.

This book is, as I have already said, being written in America, and one cannot help, in that country, being acutely aware that there are many Quakers (in fact the majority) who do not practise the form of silent worship which I have described. For historical, geographical and social reasons, which I do not wish to detail now, there grew up among American Quakers in the nineteenth century a form of worship that was programmed and led by ministers or pastors. It flourished and has spread, through the missionary zeal of these Friends, to many parts of the world, so that numerically, there are more Friends who use this way of programmed worship, with music, hymns, readings, prayers, and a prepared message or sermon, than the traditional silent type.

I am second to none in my admiration for the Christian devotion of these Quakers, and for the way in which they have carried into practise many traditional Quaker witnesses. I also recognize their worship-services as fully valid acts of worship; but at the same time I cannot help feeling that they would be making an even greater contribution to the needs of their fellow men, if alongside their programmed worship, they reintroduced the practice of quiet worship after the traditional manner of Friends.

Children and worship

One of the most admirable features of the programmed type of Quakerism is the care for their children. In any Quaker community children occupy an important role, and any Quaker meeting is greatly enriched by their presence. But how do they respond to silent Quaker worship? There was a time when Quaker children were taken to meeting and were expected to sit through it from beginning to end. At the age of 13, Richenda Gurney was quite clear about her reaction. In her journal for Sunday, December 24th 1797 she writes, 'I shall not say much of this day, as indeed it is not worth saying much about it. It was flat, stupid, unimproving and Sundayish. I spent *four* hours at meeting! I never, never wish to see that nasty hole again.'[95]

Modern Friends show more sense in the attitude to children and meeting for worship. Nowadays it is usual (as I have noted earlier) for children to attend for the opening or closing period of the meeting, generally being present for between ten and fifteen minutes. I am a strong supporter of the view that children should be in at the end rather than at the beginning of meeting. Towards its close the meeting will be at its deepest and most gathered, and children will thus feel the impact of silent worship at its best. They are by no means insensitive to its invisible power and will readily respond to it. The objection usually raised against my view is that the eruption of a group of small, lively children into meeting is an unnecessary disturbance. To this I would reply that if a meeting is profoundly gathered it can speedily absorb any interruption in its deep silence.

The reason I am not so much in favour of children being present during the opening period of the meeting is that it most

140

likely will not have achieved a deep place, so that children will only experience it while it is in the process of settling down. Further, there is likely to be a strong temptation resting on some Friends to speak to the children, which I view in any case as unfortunate, added to which it means that ministry is liable to be given early in meeting, at a time when it is not generally helpful, and least likely to arise from the life of the meeting. Children have an uncanny knack of knowing the difference between living ministry, as opposed to words that are injected into the meeting for their good. This is why I feel Friends should at any time avoid deliberately speaking to children, for it usually means speaking down to them. In fact, it is an excellent discipline for anyone who speaks in meeting to try to use words and ideas that can be understood by children, and yet speak to the condition of all present, because they arise from the profound depths which, in fact, produces things that are truly simple.

It is important to integrate children and teenagers into the life of the meeting by the simple and rewarding act of making friends with them. The only point I wish to make here relates to their full participation in the meeting for worship. Older Friends are always so glad when young people, who have grown up in the meeting, gradually take their part in it as adults. Equally, they are saddened when the opposite happens and their young rarely or never come to meeting. I am sure we should not be over-anxious about this, and certainly never bring pressure, hidden or open, upon them to come. When they, or any Friend or attender, reappear after a long period of absence many a well-meaning Friend often greets them with what is supposed to be a humorous, kindly remark of the order of 'How nice to see you—you are quite a stranger!' They will be deeply conscious of the fact that they are in the category of absentees or strangers and probably have a sense of guilt about it. So don't rub it in but be content with a simple friendly welcome. The same kind of unfortunate remark is often made to the young person who speaks in meeting for the first time. In their delight, older Friends tend to overwhelm the young person with praise and gratitude, so that he is quite embarrassed. If what he, or anyone else has said in meeting has been helpful, then again just say this simply and leave it at that.

One final comment on young people and the Society: when I was a member of Young Friends Central Committee we were discussing a subject that is a perennial one on that Committee's agenda, 'Why don't more of the children of Friends join the Society?' Edgar Castle, at that time Headmaster of Leighton Park School, wisely commented that we should wait until the person is at least 30 before we conclude that they have no further use for the Society. My observation of what happens fully justifies his comment.

Quaker weddings

There are three special forms that Quaker worship can assume in particular connection with the meeting as a community. Here I wish to restrict any comments to the particular part that silent worship plays in them. The first is Quaker weddings. A meeting for worship is specially appointed for the solemnization of marriage which ' . . . has always been regarded by Friends as a religious, not a mere civil compact'.[96] It is the only time in which any actual form of words is required to be said in a Quaker meeting. These are the promises that the partners make to one another: 'Friends, I take this my friend C.D. to be my wife, promising through divine assistance, to be unto her a loving and faithful husband, so long as we both on earth shall live.'[97] The woman then makes a similar promise. Quaker marriages are recognized in law. For our purposes the important thing to notice is the fact that, unlike ordinary

142

meetings for worship, which are general in their intention, those held in connection with a marriage do have this fact as their particular reason. So while they follow the usual course of opening with a quiet period of worship in which all present are settling into the silence; their journey to the inner side of their lives is coloured by the knowledge that during the meeting two people are going to take each other as man and wife. Quakers have always recognized that the couple concerned are taking one another in marriage in the presence of God. The Friends present do not marry them but are gathered as joyful, worshipping witnesses of this happy but solemn act. It is in the depth of their being—at the still centre—that this act of union, so charged with transcendence, takes place. It is in that same still place that Friends unite with them in prayerful compassionate thought and thankfulness for their present joy and future happiness and fulfilment. It always seems to me that those who witness this important event should also assume a responsibility, not only to the particular couple, but also to all the other couples they know, promising to do all in their power to seek to answer their prayer for support to be given to them, in whatever practical way that is open.

Naturally Quaker weddings are occasions on which a number of people are present who probably have never before attended a Quaker meeting of any kind. One cannot help being interested in the impact that this gathering makes upon them. Over and over again these visitors, mostly young, express their appreciation of the natural beauty, dignity and simplicity of the ceremony and their sense of its appropriateness.

Quaker funerals

Quaker funerals are other occasions on which many present will never have been to a Quaker meeting for worship and their remarks are not dissimilar to those made about Quaker weddings. Quakers have never considered funerals to be primarily times for mourning, although they will be sensitive to the feeling of irretrievable loss by those who are bereaved. Rather they have considered them as times when thankfulness can rightly be expressed for the grace of God expressed in the life of the deceased Friends. This attitude has been strengthened by the Quaker conviction that the real values of life transcend time and space and have about them an eternal quality.

The widespread use of cremation has brought about a change in the pattern of Quaker funerals. In times past the coffin was carried into the meeting house and a brief meeting for worship has been held before the interment which was often within the burial ground surrounding the meeting house.

Nowadays it is more usual for the family and a few Friends to share in a meeting for worship at the crematorium. Later a memorial meeting for worship may be held in the meeting house. The particular reason for gathering affects the nature of the worship, although, as always in any Quaker meeting, it consists in a quiet centring down in stillness. Any ministry given will avoid mere eulogy of the deceased person, and seek to see in his life those signals of transcendence that point to the eternal values that give to life its meaning and purpose. Once again there is laid on all who are present the responsibility to translate their prayers for comfort and support into thoughtful, kindly and sustained actions that will continue to help those who have lost a loved one to face life anew with courage, and to adapt themselves to their new circumstances.

Quaker business meetings

The third and final way in which Quaker worship is closely linked with the life of the Quaker community is the major part it plays in those gatherings in which its business is conducted. These can be at the local, district or national level. Again our only concern is with the actual role of worship in these meetings. They all open with a period of quiet waiting in which a corporate journey can be made to the still centre from where alone true decisions can be made. Again the intention of the gathering affects its worship, for practical issues calling for unity in decision is the main reason for them. Quakers seek to reach their decisions without voting, for Quaker business meetings are theocratic rather than democratic, and they seek to achieve this by giving the freedom for all present to express their view if they feel drawn to do so. The way in which they do this will be similar to the way in which ministry arises in an ordinary meeting for worship. It will we hope not be an ill-thought-through contribution tossed lightly off the top of the mind, but one that arises from the deep centre of life. Of course, one must keep matters in proportion, for there are some decisions that can be quickly and easily reached without any profound exercise on the part of the meeting. But there will be others of such importance that they call for a most searching exploration in the depths of being, and even when this has been faithfully carried out it may not be possible for the meeting to achieve unity. On such occasions the wisdom and experience of the Society urge that no decision should be taken, it being better to delay action than to compromise in a judgement which does not represent a unity known and felt by all in the depth of the meeting's life. I have learnt by long experience that it is extremely unwise to make dogmatic statements about Quaker behaviour: however, I am perfectly prepared to be dogmatic about the fact that, if a decision overrides the sincere and strongly held convictions of a number of those present, then sooner or later it will be found to have been faulty.

Despite the fact that Quaker business meetings are held on the continuing basis of worship, Friends are human enough to get, from time to time, into what the Americans expressively call a 'hassle'. At such times an argumentative spirit can arise that quickly destroys the atmosphere of worship. On such occasions it is usual for the Clerk to call for a period of quiet worship. It is interesting, if not surprising, in view of what I have already said about the nature of Quaker worship, how this quiet, still pause can bring about a real search for unity which frequently results in the achievement of actual unity. It is then the duty of the Clerk to record the decision reached in the form of a written minute, that is open for amendment and acceptance, and so is recognized as the will of God for Friends in that matter. More often than not this is what happens. But Friends' business meetings, like their meetings for worship, sometimes fall short of the ideal. I said earlier that the worst state into which the latter can fall is to degenerate to the level of a poor debating society. The worst state into which a Quaker meeting for business can fall is to settle a controversial issue by degenerating to a majority 'shout'. By this I mean that the Clerk, having read his minute, which is still obviously not accepted by some seriously concerned Friends present, allows the majority of Friends present to chorus some such phrase as 'I approve'. In those circumstances the meeting has lost its deep centre and to my mind it would be more honest to delay a decision rather than to use the voices of the majority in the form of a vote, which is repugnant to the Society, as it is a method by which the majority can ride rough-shod over the view of the minority. In any case I am sure this device is not necessary; for by patient, quiet and prolonged search in depth, all Quaker experience points to the fact that a truly unified decision can be reached. But I agree it tests most severely our trust in the amazing fact of Quaker worship.

All true Quaker action has its origins in the quiet seeking and life of Quaker worship, and the Society always fails on those rare occasions when action is taken that does not arise from this deep life, usually because of the pressure of a particular group. From time to time true Quaker action has arisen outside the normal business structure of the Society and has finally won acceptance because its origins were clearly grounded in the life at the deep centre. This, however, should be recognized as exceptional, and the Society wisely seeks to channel its decision-making through the machinery it has set up at the local and district levels, in Preparative, Monthly and General Meetings, and through Meeting for Sufferings and Yearly Meeting at the national level.

THE AMAZING FACT OF QUAKER WORSHIP

Some Friends are able to recall with clarity the first occasion on which they attended a Quaker meeting. While I cannot remember when or where I did so, I do have a vivid recollection of the meeting which I began to attend regularly.

It was held in a rather hideous building: the meeting room was dingy. We sat on rickety chairs that creaked at the slightest movement. The whole place gave little hope that those who worshipped there might catch a glimpse of the vision of God. It was in stark contrast to the splendour of the Anglican churches to which I had been accustomed, where through dignified ritual the beauty of holiness was vividly portrayed.

However, it was in this unlikely setting that I came to know what I can only describe as the amazing fact of Quaker worship. It was in that uncomfortable room that I discovered the way to the interior side of my life, at the deep centre of which I knew that I was not alone, but was held by a love that passes all understanding. This love was mediated to me, in the first place, by those with whom I worshipped. For my journey was not solitary, but one undertaken with my friends as we moved towards each other and together travelled inwards. Yet I knew that the love that held me could not be limited to the mutual love and care we had for each other. It was a signal of transcendence that pointed beyond itself to the source of all life and love.

In that ordinary room a group of ordinary people entered quietly into a new dimension in which everyday life was transformed and transcended, as we found a depth of loving communion that was infinite and eternal in its quality. This was achieved by waiting together in stillness without the assistance of a trained leadership, ritual acts or programmed worship.

There was a remarkable sense of freedom among us for we were not bound by dogma nor restricted by the negative side of credal statements. At the same time we were supported by a strong awareness of trust in life as having meaning and purpose. Our experience drew from us the conviction that love was the nature of this meaning and purpose.

The experience could be described at many levels, and interpreted in many ways. At the lowest it could be seen as a human activity and expressed in secular language. At the highest it could be seen as the breaking in of divinity to be described in transcendent or religious language. The range of outlook and attitudes held by the group was wide. The experience of individuals varied enormously. At the extreme poles it would seem that the one must contradict the other—yet at the still centre we found unity not conflict.

Some of the people in the meeting would speak naturally of the power of the spirit silently at work sharing the harvest of ' . . . love, joy, peace, patience, kindness, goodness, fidelity, gentleness, and self-control.'[98] Some would speak of the presence of Christ in the midst bringing the strength of his redeeming love. Some would find it more natural to use impersonal language and to speak of a stream of consciousness or some such words.

The range of interpretation was not dissimilar to that represented by Alistair Kee and Peter Berger whose books I have quoted earlier. The former sees Christ as disclosing a way of transcendence to be described in purely secular terms. The latter seeks for signals of transcendence by which modern society may re-discover the supernatural.

A gateway to transcendence

All life was present in that shabby room which Sunday after Sunday was silently transformed into a gateway to transcendence. Together we knew the simple happiness of living: the essential goodness and meaning of life. Together we experienced moments of despair and depression when truth, love and goodness seemed to be obliterated by the evil in ourselves and in the world around us. But terrifying as were those black periods when ' . . . there was an ocean of darkness and death', we, like George Fox also saw ' . . . an infinite ocean of light and love, which flowed over the ocean of darkness.'[99] Also like George Fox we saw in the darkness and the light 'the infinite love of God'. For all of us had looked at our world and had been drawn to interpret its meaning as love. To this interpretation we had committed ourselves and by its light we tried to live.

The experience of my first encounter with Quaker worship was not misleading. It has been repeated over and over again in countless other meetings I have known. Sometimes I have come across Friends and others who feel that to interpret religious experience basically in terms of love is too simple and easy. Religion, they say, is something that makes fundamental claims upon our obedience. All I can say in reply is that to love another person really and in depth is the hardest demand that can be made upon us. It transcends all law and moral obligation and calls for a response from the whole of our personality. It is a costly, sacrificial activity, the true nature of which was dramatically shown by the death of Jesus on the cross.

The more we respond in love to others and accept their love for us, the greater our capacity for love becomes. This extraordinary character of love which is inherently creative urges us to see that love is the meaning, truth and reality of life. At this point we find ourselves responding warmly to the developing awareness of the nature of God recorded in the pages of the Bible which culminated in the explicit New Testament statement that God is love.

Quakerism is essentially empirical rather than theoretical in its approach to religion. Quakers come to it not by way of argument about transcendence or love or the existence of God, but by putting themselves in a position where they can be open to experience. So the essential life of the Society of Friends is to be seen in the repeated activity of worship. Here Quakers continually re-affirm the worth of love, and through dwelling silently in the presence of this love, know the presence of God, not as theory but as fact. I recall some words of William Temple contrasting his experience of listening to music with that of his experience of worship. After a concert he wished to be undisturbed so that he could continue to enjoy the music. After worship he wanted to be with people so that he could share with and receive from them the love that filled his heart.

In the seventeenth century Robert Barclay described his experience of worship by saying, ' . . . when I came into the silent assemblies of God's people, I felt a secret power among them, which touched my heart; and as I gave way unto it I found the evil weakening in me and the good raised up . . . '.[100] In the twentieth century we can identify this 'secret power' most readily with the creative power of love. The interpretations we make of this experience will vary greatly as will the ways in which we respond to its overwhelming demands. In worship we recognize that love is the most truly human of all human experience, while at the same time it is something that is given to us so that we can face its demands with joyful confidence.

However we interpret the experience of love in the still centre of our being, and its deepest disclosure to us all in the communion of worship, we may not find words that can express it

more adequately than those of St. Paul. 'For I am convinced',
he wrote 'that there is nothing in death or life, in the realm of
spirits or superhuman powers, in the world as it is or the world
as it shall be, in the forces of the universe, in heights or depths
—nothing in all creation that can separate us from the love of
God in Christ Jesus our Lord.'[101]

REFERENCES

[1] Berger (Peter L.) *A Rumour of Angels: modern society and the rediscovery of the supernatural.* London: Penguin, 1971, p. 10.

[2] *Ibid.*, p. 70.

[3] *Ibid.*, p. 70.

[4] *Ibid.*, p. 75.

[5] *Ibid.*, p. 75.

[6] *Ibid.*, pp. 75–6.

[7] Hodgkin (L. Violet) *Silent Worship: the way of wonder.* Swarthmore Lecture. London: Swarthmore Press, 1919, p. 64.

[8] Fox (George) *Doctrinals* (1657) quoted by Gladys Wilson in *Quaker Worship.* London: Bannisdale, 1952, p. 13.

[9] Robert Barclay (1648–1690) quoted by L. V. Hodgkin, *op. cit.*, p. 57.

[10] Huxley (Aldous) *The Perennial Philosophy.* London: Chatto, 1946, p. 249.

[11] Lamb (Charles) 'A Quaker's Meeting' in *The Essays of Elia.* World Classics. London: Oxford University Press, 1946.

[12] From a letter of George Fox to Lady Claypole (1658) quoted in Nickalls (J. L.) ed., *The Journal of George Fox.* London: Cambridge University Press, 1952, p. 346.

[13] Penn (William) *Fruits of a Father's Love* (1726) quoted by L. V. Hodgkin, *op. cit.*, p. 61.

[14] Meynell (Wilfred) ed. *Poetical Works of Francis Thompson.* London: Oxford University Press, 1937, p. 92.

[15] Huxley (Julian) *Essays of a Humanist.* London: Chatto, 1964, p. 112.

[16] Murdoch (Iris) *The Sovereignty of Good.* London: Routledge, 1970.

[17] Robert Barclay quoted by Howard Collier in *The Quaker Meeting.* London: Friends Home Service Committee 1949, p. 18.

[18] Story (Thomas) *Journal* (1747) quoted in *Christian Faith and Practice in the Experience of the Society of Friends.* London Yearly Meeting of the Religious Society of Friends, 1960, §44.

[19] Penington (Isaac) *Works* (1679) quoted by Gladys Wilson, *op. cit.*, p. 43.

[20] Keith (George) *The Benefits, Advantage, and Glory of Silent Meetings* (1670), quoted by Gladys Wilson, *op. cit.*, p. 43.

[21] Hammarskjöld (Dag) *Markings.* London: Faber, 1964.

[22] Lee (R. S.) *Psychology and Worship.* London: SCM, 1955, p. 80.

[23] Jones (Rufus M.) 'The Spiritual Message of the Religious Society of Friends' in Report of Commission I of the First World Conference of Friends (1937) quoted in *Christian Faith and Practice*, § 244.

[24] Eliot (T. S.) 'Burnt Norton' in *Four Quartets.* London: Faber, 1944, p. 14.

[25] Keith, *op. cit.*, quoted by L. Violet Hodgkin, *op. cit.*, p. 88.

155

[16] Francis Howgill (1618–1669) quoted in *Christian Faith and Practice*, § 184.

[17] Barclay (Robert) *Apology* (1676) quoted by Gladys Wilson, *op. cit.*, p. 45.

[18] Penington (Isaac) *Works* (1679) quoted by Gladys Wilson, *op. cit.*, p. 41.

[19] Thomas Story (1662–1742) quoted in *Christian Faith and Practice*, § 44.

[30] Kee (Alistair) *The Way of Transcendence*. London: Penguin, 1971, p. 5.

[31] *Ibid.*, p. 5.

[32] Doncaster (L. Hugh) *The Quaker Message: a personal affirmation*. James Backhouse Lecture. Wallingford, Pennsylvania: Pendle Hill Pamphlet 181, 1972, p. 12.

[33] *Ibid.*, p. 5.

[34] Kee, *op. cit.*, p. xvi.

[35] *Ibid.*, p. 8.

[36] *Ibid.*, p. 4.

[37] *Ibid.*, p. 11.

[38] *Ibid.*, p. 18.

[39] Berger, *op cit.*, p. 70.

[40] *Ibid.*, p. 71.

[41] Bliss (Kathleen) *The Future of Religion*. London: Penguin, 1972, p. 145.

[42] Williams (Harry) *True Resurrection*. London: Mitchell Beazley, 1972, p. 70–1.

[43] Spinks (Stephen) *Psychology and Religion*. London: Methuen, 1962, p. 176.

[44] Macquarrie (John) *Paths in Spirituality*. London: SCM, 1972.

[45] Bliss, *op. cit.*, p. 134.

[46] *Church Government*. London Yearly Meeting of the Religious Society of Friends, 1968, § 702.

[47] Williams (Harry) *The True Wilderness*. London: Penguin, 1968, pp. 32–3.

[48] Penn (William) Preface to George Fox's *Journal* (1694) quoted in *Christian Faith and Practice*, § 183.

[49] Macquarrie, *op. cit.*, p. 30.

[50] *Ibid.*, p. 71.

[51] Green (Thomas) *Preparation for Worship*. Swarthmore Lecture, 1952. London: Friends Home Service Committee, 1964, p. 23.

[52] Lacout (Pierre) *God is silence*. London: Friends Home Service Committee, 1970, p. 8.

[53] Berger, *op. cit.*, p. 108.

[54] Lacout, *op. cit.*, p. 4.

[55] Nickalls (J. L.) ed. *The Journal of George Fox*. London: Cambridge University Press, 1952, p. 4.

[56] Jones (Rufus M.) *Studies in Mystical Religion*. London: Macmillan, 1909, p. xxxviii.

REFERENCES

[57] Brinton (Howard H.) *Creative Worship and Other Essays*. Walling-ford, Pennsylvania: Pendle Hill, 1957, p. v.

[58] Collier (Howard E.) *The Quaker Meeting*. London: Friends Home Service Committee, 1949, p. 4.

[59] Lacout, *op. cit.*, p. 9.

[60] Berger, *op. cit.*, p. 112.

[61] Macmurray (John) *Beyond Knowledge*. London: Macmillan, 1927, pp. 28–9.

[62] Bliss, *op. cit.*, p. 155.

[63] Kee, *op. cit.*, p. 16.

[64] *Ibid.*, p. 16.

[65] Solzhenitsyn (Alexander) *August 1914*. London: Bodley Head, 1972, p. 80.

[66] Lacout, *op. cit.*, p. 4.

[67] Underhill (Evelyn) *Worship*. 3rd edn. London: Nisbet, 1937, p. 313.

[68] Stephen (Caroline) *Light Arising* (1908) quoted in *Christian Faith and Practice*, § 246.

[69] Hodgkin, *op. cit.*, p. 64.

[70] Green, *op. cit.*, p. 12.

[71] Isaac Penington (1616--1679) quoted by L. Violet Hodgkin, *op. cit.* p. 62.

[72] Barclay (Robert) *An Apology for the True Christian Divinity* . . . 1676, p. 229.

[73] *Ibid.*, p. 226.

[74] *Ibid.*, p. 226.

[75] Story (Thomas) *Life* (1693), quoted by Gladys Wilson, *op. cit.*, p. 54.

[76] Penington (Isaac) *Works* (1679) quoted by Gladys Wilson, *op. cit.*, p. 32.

[77] Graham (J. W.) *The Quaker Ministry*. London: Swarthmore Press, 1925, p. 44.

[78] Kelly (Thomas) *Reality of the Spiritual World* (1942) and *The Gathered Meeting* (1941). London: Friends Home Service Committee, 1965, p. 49.

[79] Berger, *op. cit.*, p. 110.

[80] Williams (Harry) *The True Wilderness*. London: Penguin, 1968, pp. 32–3.

[81] Green, *op. cit.*, p. 23.

[82] Bliss, *op. cit.*, p. 164.

[83] Kelly, *op. cit.*, p. 43.

[84] Green, *op. cit.*, p. 23.

[85] Hodgkin, *op. cit.*, p. 77.

[86] Fox (George) *Epistles*, 1698. Ep. 150 (1657).

[87] Story (Thomas) *Journal* (1747), quoted by William C. Braithwaite *The Second Period of Quakerism*. 2nd edn. revised by Henry Cadbury. London: Cambridge University Press, 1961, p. 545.

[88] Bownas (Samuel) *Qualifications Necessary to a Gospel Minister* (1750) quoted by Gladys Wilson, *op. cit.*, p. 57.

[89] Fox (George) *Epistles*, 1698. Ep. 150 (1657).

[90] *Church Government*, § 704.
[91] Graham, *op. cit.*, p. 26.
[92] Lacout, *op. cit.*, p. 2.
[93] *Church Government*, § 703.
[94] Smith (Stevie) 'Not waving but drowning' in *Penguin Modern Poets, Book 8*. London: Penguin, 1970, p. 100.
[95] From Richenda Gurney's *Journal*, quoted by Augustus Hare in *The Gurneys of Earlham*. London: George Allen, 1895, p, 70.
[96] *Christian Faith and Practice*, § 486.
[97] *Church Government*, § 906.
[98] *Galatians*, v, 22.
[99] Nickalls, *op. cit.*, p. 27.
[100] Barclay, *op. cit.*, p. 255.
[101] *Romans*, viii, 38–9.